Exalted LORD

A Study of JESUS CHRIST'S Exaltation from the Book of Acts

RANDAL L. GILMORE

Exalted
LORD

A Study of
JESUS CHRIST'S Exaltation
from the Book of Acts

RANDAL L. GILMORE

EXALT Publications
Fishers, Indiana
www.exaltpublications.com

ISBN: 9780978773267

TABLE OF CONTENTS

DEDICATION

*Dedicated to my precious Lord, Jesus Christ,
exalted at the Father's right hand.*

EXALTED LORD RESOURCES

*A complementary Exalted Lord musical CD featuring Christian artists Amy and Patrick Fata
is also available on iTunes. Lyrics excerpted from the CD appear
at the beginning of each chapter.*

ACKNOWLEDGEMENTS

*A debt of gratitude is owed to Dick and Anne Busch for their generous support
of the entire Exalted Lord project. May our Lord bless your investments in ministry
with abundant and everlasting fruit for His glory!
Many thanks also to Amy and Patrick Fata for their creativity in putting to music the themes
of each chapter in such a Christ-honoring way.
Finally, much appreciation rightfully goes to Lisa Illig of OliveTeapot.Com
for the artistry of the Exalted Lord book and CD covers.*

PREFACE

Every true Christian believes that Jesus died, was buried, and rose again. As important as these events are, they do not tell the whole story of Jesus. Following the resurrection, Jesus appeared on earth for forty days. On day forty, He ascended into heaven to sit down at the right hand of God the Father. Jesus' enthronement at the Father's right hand marked the beginning of His exaltation as Lord of lords. His exaltation will culminate in His literal, bodily return to the earth, at which time He will utterly rout all of His enemies, making them His footstool.

Presently, as our High Priest, Jesus is interceding for everyone who has believed on Him. As the exalted Lord of lords, Jesus also serves as a mighty general, orchestrating events that will lead someday to His enemies' utter defeat. Accordingly, even in the darkest of circumstances, we can be sure that the mighty Lord Jesus remains in control. He will win in the end. In the meantime, Jesus provides grace, power, meaning, and a sense of His presence so we might share in His victories.

A study of the Book of Acts reveals the impact God intends for Jesus' exaltation as Lord to have on people in life here and now. My own encounter with that impact began when I first believed on Jesus as an eight year-old boy. It then took an even more profound hold on my life several years ago as I was preparing a series of sermons on the Book of Acts for my church. Until that time, I had studied and taught through Acts based on the themes of the Church and the Holy Spirit, both of which are featured prominently throughout the book. Then I made two decisions that changed forever the way I look at what Luke wrote. The first was to approach my study of Acts from a narrative perspective. The second was to purchase and read "The Character and Purpose of Luke's Christology" by Douglas Buckwalter. Buckwalter's book is a careful and scholarly analysis of the themes of Luke's Gospel and the Book of Acts. The more I read and reflected on Buckwalter's insights, the more I began to see Acts' theme of "Jesus as the exalted Lord."

These decisions not only changed the way I looked at Luke's writings, they also changed my understanding of numerous other associated passages of Scripture. They also changed my life. Many times since, I have said to myself and to anyone else who would listen: "How could we have missed this!"

The "Exalted Lord" study you are about to read is just a small piece of the fruit God has produced in my heart and mind as I continue to make my way through Luke-Acts and the rest of the New Testament. I must emphasize this study is not just another salvo for one side or the other in the so-called "Lordship salvation" debate. Much of the discussion on both sides of that debate misses the profound and life-changing significance of Jesus' exaltation. As the realization sinks in of who Jesus is as the exalted Lord and Christ, not only do people embrace Him by faith, they also begin to treasure Him. They begin to count every experience of gain apart from Him as nothing but loss. They start living for the purpose of knowing Him and the power of His resurrection. From the depths of their being, they begin to marshal and manage all of their resources to be instruments of His Lordship.

Many Christians will recognize the Philippians 3 language toward the end of the last paragraph. Since I embarked on the study you are about to read, I began to recognize the reality of Philippians 3:7-14 in my own heart and life. I stress that I am just beginning and have not yet "apprehended that for which I have been apprehended." Accordingly, I press on, and I invite you now to join me.

1

Exalted Lord, reigning high
Over earth, over sky,
Exalted King, on Your Throne,
Glorious grace and mercy shown,

Exalted Christ, crucified,
Defeating death to bring us life,
Savior, Friend, so much more,
Exalted Lord.

Lyrics from "Exalted Lord"
by Amy Branson Fata

Paul's Encounter with the Exalted Lord

Saul of Taurus stood near Gamaliel, one of the Sanhedrin's most revered Pharisees, listening intently to his teacher's insights on what to do about the apostles and their teaching in Jesus' Name. "Men of Israel," Gamaliel began, "take care what you are about to do with these men. For before these days Theudas rose up, claiming to be somebody, and a number of men, about four hundred, joined him. He was killed, and all who followed him were dispersed and came to nothing."[1]

Gamaliel knew what he was talking about. Near the end of the first century A.D., a Jewish historian, who went by the Roman name of Flavius Josephus, wrote about Theudas and Judas the Galilean in a history of the Jews entitled, "Jewish Antiquities". Josephus recounted how Theudas, whom he calls a charlatan, influenced a large group of people to gather their belongings and follow him to the Jordan River.[2] Theudas claimed he would be able to divide the river, like Joshua of old, and that everyone would be able to cross over on dry ground. However, the Roman Procurator Fadus dispatched a garrison of soldiers to intercept Theudas and his band. The soldiers ruthlessly slaughtered most of them. As for Theudas, the soldiers severed his head. They then fashioned it into a kind of trophy and carried it triumphantly back to Jerusalem.

Judas the Galilean also met with an unhappy end after taking on a similar pseudo-messianic mission. Judas and his followers launched a rebellion against a census ordered by a Roman governor named Coponius, believing the census to be a precursor of yet another unbearable tax. No one knows exactly how much of a fight Judas and his followers waged. We do know they failed miserably. They didn't stop the census, nor did they escape with their lives.

Which figures from recent history are considered by many to have had a messiah-like following?

What characteristics do most false messiahs share?

Saul the Persecutor

Though Gamaliel could have strengthened his argument before the Sanhedrin with the names and stories of numerous other would-be messiahs, the situation did not require it. The case of the ordinary, uneducated fishermen standing in front of them now differed little from that of the followers of Theudas and Judas the Galilean. The fishermen were simply the latest to be caught up with a would-be messiah. It was true they had filled Jerusalem with certain outrageous claims about Jesus of Nazareth, including accusations against the Sanhedrin for murdering him.[3] They also had foolishly asserted that God raised Jesus from the dead and "exalted him at his right hand as Leader and Savior."[4] Still Gamaliel advised, "Keep away from these men and let them alone, for if this plan or this undertaking is of man, it will fail; but if it is of God, you will not be able to overthrow them. You might even be found opposing God!"[5]

Gamaliel's words, although persuasive, failed to connect with the heart of Saul, the teacher's most promising student and fellow member of the Sanhedrin. Saul could not stomach even the suggestion that Peter and John's message might be true. If the deaths of other would-be messiahs and their followers proved they had not come from God, then he, Saul, would be happy to set the record straight in this case. Looking back to describe his frame of mind that day, Saul confessed: "I myself was convinced that I ought to do many things in opposing the name of Jesus of Nazareth."[6]

Saul began his obsessive campaign against Jesus of Nazareth as a kind of cheerleader for others bent on executing Stephen, a Hellenist leader of the Way.[7] Stephen rose to prominence after he, along with six others, were authorized in place of the Apostles to ensure equitable distributions of food to needy widows. But the breadth of Stephen's ministry eventually surpassed the task originally assigned to him. He began doing "great wonders and signs among the people."[8] And he spoke effectively in defense of Jesus' Lordship, anchoring his arguments in Jewish history and law dating back to Moses. When Stephen's opponents took up stones to silence him, Saul gave his consent and volunteered to guard their outer garments.

According to Acts 7:51-53, how did Stephen characterize his persecutors (including Saul)? How did he characterize their treatment of Jesus?

Which characterizations might apply to people today who reject Jesus?

What conclusions about Jesus did Stephen want Saul and his other persecutors to draw on the basis of his statement in Acts 7:56?

A Dramatic Change

Emboldened by their initial triumph, Stephen's persecutors turned to direct their bloodlust to the rest of the followers of the Way. As a result, all "except the Apostles" fled from Jerusalem for their lives.[9] Saul stopped watching coats to join the chase: "Entering house after house, he dragged off men and women and committed them to prison."[10] Saul went "to all the synagogues" to punish any followers of the Way he could find.[11] Almost overnight, the persecution's cheerleader became the persecution's ringleader. Soon word of a Christian safe house in Damascus reached Saul's ears. Damascus, one of the ten cities of the Decapolis, enjoyed a steady flow of commercial traffic in and out. A sizable population of Jews had settled there, even though they were quite far from Jerusalem. Saul immediately recognized the danger of allowing any followers of the Way to enjoy safe haven in such a strategic city, and so "he went to the high priest and asked for letters" to take them as prisoners to Jerusalem.[12] Saul then set out for Damascus, "breathing threats and murder against the disciples of the Lord."[13]

But something unusual happened on Saul's way to Damascus: "suddenly a light from heaven flashed around him."[14] Blinded, Saul fell prostrate "to the ground."[15] When he got up, the men who were traveling with him had to lead him by the hand the rest of the way into the city. "For three days he was without sight, and neither ate nor drank."[16]

By the end of the three days, Saul's life had changed dramatically. He willingly turned his back on everything he had previously clung to for meaning, self-worth, and a standing with God. Carefully read Saul's own words:

"If anyone else thinks he has reason for confidence in the flesh, I have more: circumcised on the eighth day, of the people of Israel, of the tribe of Benjamin, a Hebrew of Hebrews; as to the law, a Pharisee; as to zeal, a persecutor of the church; as to righteousness under the law, blameless. But whatever gain I had, I counted as loss for the sake of Christ. Indeed, I count everything as loss because of the surpassing worth of knowing Christ Jesus my Lord. For his sake I have suffered the loss of all

*things and count them as rubbish, in order that I may gain Christ
and be found in him, not having a righteousness of my own that
comes from the law, but that which comes through faith in Christ, the
righteousness from God that depends on faith—that I may know him
and the power of his resurrection, and may share his sufferings, becoming like him in his death, that by any means possible I may attain the
resurrection from the dead. Not that I have already obtained this or
am already perfect, but I press on to make it my own, because Christ
Jesus made me his own. Brothers, I do not consider that I have made it
my own. But one thing I do: forgetting what lies behind and straining
forward to what lies ahead, I press on toward the goal for the prize of
the upward call of God in Christ Jesus."[17]*

*Throughout these verses, Saul uses the language of an investor.
What "investments" had Saul included in his life's portfolio
prior to seeing Jesus on the Damascus Road?*

*What "investments" are you including right now
in the "portfolio" of your own life?*

Jesus Is Alive!

On the road to Damascus, the exalted Lord Jesus spoke
to Saul out of the blazing, brilliant light flashing from heaven
around him and his companions: "Saul, Saul, why are you persecuting me?"

"Who are you, Lord?" Saul asked somewhat confused at first.
"I am Jesus, whom you are persecuting," came the unmistakably
clear reply.[18]

Though simple, this exchange sent Saul's heart and mind
racing. He had known beyond any doubt or contradiction that

Jesus of Nazareth had been executed in Jerusalem; "for this has not been done in a corner," he once said to King Agrippa.[19] Seeing Jesus now, obviously exalted and in such brilliant light, meant the fishermen were right after all! Jesus is alive! God had raised him from the dead!

The implications overwhelmed Saul: "Resurrection from the dead! How incredible!" From this moment forward, the resurrection of Jesus began to occupy a central place in Saul's thinking. When he faced persecution of his own toward the end of his life and ministry, he boldly declared to the authorities: "Brothers, I am a Pharisee, a son of Pharisees. It is with respect to the hope and the resurrection from the dead that I am on trial."[20]

Light and darkness became Saul's favorite metaphors for explaining what happened in his own heart that day. Look up the following Scriptures in which light is used as a metaphor for conversion or salvation. Summarize what each contributes to our understanding of Saul's experience:

Acts 26:18

2 Corinthians 6:14

Acts 26:23

2 Corinthians 11:14

Romans 2:19

Ephesians 5:8-14

Romans 13:12

Colossians 1:12

1 Corinthians 3:13; 4:5

1 Thessalonians 5:5

2 Corinthians 4:4-6

2 Timothy 1:10

Based on what you know of Saul's life prior to his experience on the road to Damascus, what would you say it means to live in spiritual darkness?

How do the following verses connect the resurrection of Jesus with his exaltation?

Acts 5:31-32

Acts 5:29-32

Acts 10:39-43

1 Corinthians 15:1-28

Colossians 3:1

Jesus the Highly Exalted Christ of God

Soon many other things began falling into place in Saul's mind. Saul realized he had seen the One for whom all of history had been waiting and in whom all of history would one day be fulfilled. He had seen the Lord in the brilliant light of His exaltation. To Saul, who later became known as Paul, the title, Lord, was much more than just an ordinary title of respect: "It was the most adequate term for expressing what he (and his fellow-believers) had come to understand and appreciate of Jesus' person and achievement and His present decisive role in the outworking of God's purpose of blessing for the universe."[21]

Paul came to believe that Jesus of Nazareth truly is the highly exalted Christ of God. Yes, Jesus had suffered and died. Yes, He had been buried. But He rose again on the third day. Soon after, He ascended to the right hand of the Father, where He was gloriously enthroned. Once Paul believed in Jesus, his life changed forever, as will the life of everyone who makes the same heart-deep confession of faith in Him.[22]

Before you began this study, what came to your mind when you read or heard the title "Lord" used in reference to Jesus?

At this point in the study, what would you say to others to summarize what "Lord" means?

What Bible verses used in this chapter stand out the most to you?

Now that you completed Chapter 1, describe how you hope God might use this study in your life?

Try restating your answer to the previous question in the form of a prayer.

1 Acts 5:36 **2** Josephus **3** Acts 5:28 **4** Acts 5:30-31 **5** Acts 5:38-39 **6** Acts 26:9 **7** See Acts 9:2; 19:9, 23; 22:4; and 24:14, 22. In the first century A.D., followers of Jesus became known as followers of "the Way" before they became known as "Christians". **8** Acts 6:8 **9** Acts 8:1 **10** Acts 8:3 **11** Acts 26:11 **12** Acts 9:1-2 **13** Acts 9:1 **14** Acts 9:3 **15** Acts 9:4 **16** Acts 9:9 **17** Philippians 3:4-14 **18** Acts 9-4-5 **19** Acts 26:26 **20** Acts 23:6 **21** Bruce, F.F. (1977). Paul Apostle of the Heart Set Free. Grand Rapids: Wm. B. Erdmann's Publishing Co., 117 **22** See Roman 10:9-10

Exalted LORD

With basin in hand, You bent to the floor
Washing their feet, a servant's chore
You were not the king
they thought You would be
No robe, no crown, no majesty

You bent the knee with me in mind
Humility, the purest kind
King of kings serving man
You bent the knee so I could stand

Lyrics from "You Bent the Knee"
by Amy Branson Fata

2

THIS SAME JESUS

Theologians sometimes use the expression "the historical Jesus" to stand for all that Jesus did and taught and for all that happened to Him from His conception in Mary's womb until the resurrection. They use "the exalted Jesus" to describe who Jesus became once He rose again, ascended into heaven, and sat down at God's right hand.

When the two ways of referring to Jesus are grounded in the truth of Scripture, they do not mean there is more than one Jesus.[1] Instead, they signify more than one category for understanding exactly who and what Jesus is. Jesus lived on earth as an historical person. Following His death, He was raised to new life and exalted as Lord. In spite of differences between the two categories, there is only one Jesus. The Jesus exalted as Lord is the same Jesus who lived historically.

Jesus Himself spoke of both categories. He plainly declared: "I came from the Father and have come into the world," a reference to the historical category of His experience.[2] Jesus also referred to the category of His exaltation when He stood before the council of elders and announced just prior to being sent to Pilate for crucifixion: "But from now on the Son of Man shall be seated at the right hand of the power of God."[3]

The Humiliation of the Historical Jesus

In his Gospel account, Luke purposefully and repeatedly calls attention to the "historical" Jesus and His humility. Luke's emphasis leads to our understanding of Jesus' conception, birth, earthly existence, suffering, and death as His humiliation.

Luke begins his Gospel by surrounding the story of Jesus' conception and birth with illustration after illustration of humility. First come Zechariah and Elizabeth, an obscure and humble couple, chosen to bear the forerunner of the Christ. Next is Mary, the mother of Jesus, who with her own lips delivers a well-known refrain of humility: "My soul magnifies the Lord and my spirit rejoices in God my Savior, for he has looked on the humble estate of his servant."[4] Then Luke brings in the shepherds, some of the more lowly citizens of Israel, as the first to visit the Christ-child, lying in the feeding trough of a stable. Feeding troughs and stables would be humble circumstances for the birth of any baby, much less the Son of God.

The poverty of Mary and Joseph stands as yet another indication of humility in association with Jesus' birth. We know of their poverty because of the sacrifice they offered when they presented Jesus in the Temple. The Law required the mother of a newborn to offer "a lamb a year-old."[5] However, "if she cannot afford a lamb, then she shall take two turtledoves or two pigeons, one for a burnt offering and the other for a sin offering."[6] Luke intentionally recalls how Mary and Joseph offered their sacrifice in accord with the Law's provision for the poor.[7]

Read through Luke chapters 1 and 2. What other indications of humility do you find in the circumstances related to Jesus' birth?

How does what is said about people like John the Baptist, Simeon, and Anna also contribute to the theme of humility?

A Powerful Example

As his Gospel moves on, Luke continues the emphasis on humility. He even records Jesus Himself articulating this theme in a declaration to the Pharisees: "For everyone who exalts himself will be humbled, but the one who humbles himself will be exalted."[8]

The humiliation of Jesus resulted in our forgiveness, but it was intended also to serve as a powerful example of how we should live. When the Apostle Paul wrote of Jesus' humiliation in his letter to the Philippians, he introduced the subject with these words: "Have this mind among yourselves, which is yours in Christ Jesus."[9] The idea is not to imitate Jesus by being born in a stable or even by dying on a cross. Imitating Jesus means humbling ourselves before God, becoming His servants and submitting to His will. It means eagerly playing the lowliest part in full expectation that someday He will lift us up. The Apostle Peter expressed it this way: "Humble yourselves, therefore, under the mighty hand of God, so that at the proper time he may exalt you."[10]

2 Samuel 22:28	*Psalm 147:6*
2 Chronicles 7:14	*Psalm 149:4*
2 Chronicles 33:23	*Proverbs 3:34*
Psalm 18:27	*Isaiah 66:2*

Heart and Will Closely Connected

The humiliation of the historical Jesus offends some people. Simeon, one of the persons mentioned in Luke's account of Jesus' birth, said as much while holding the baby Jesus in his arms: "This child is appointed for the fall and rising of many in Israel, and to be a sign that is opposed...so that thoughts from many hearts may be revealed."[11]

Simeon's words underscore the close connection between the thoughts of the heart and a person's will. Whatever lives in someone's heart shows itself in what that person wills to think, say, and do. For example, the Psalmist wrote: "My heart says to you, 'Your face, Lord, do I seek."[12] In other words, "I will seek the face of the Lord, because it is in my heart to do so."

The Apostle Paul told the Philippians that one day "every knee should bow...and every tongue confess that Jesus Christ is Lord, to the glory of God the Father."[13] Those whose hearts are full of faith in Jesus now are not willing to wait until that day to humble themselves in this way. Their hearts move them to make the confession now in accord with Paul's explanation to the Romans:

"If you confess with your mouth that Jesus is Lord and believe in your heart that God raised him from the dead, you will be saved. For with the heart one believes and is justified, and with the mouth one confesses and is saved."[14]

Read Matthew 15:10-20. How does this teaching describe the role that the heart plays in regard to a person's behavior and moral choices?

What other Scripture verses refer to the role of the heart in spiritual matters or moral choices? (Use a concordance or Bible software if necessary). Which of these verses stand out to you? Why ?

What is your heart telling you now to humbly confess about Jesus?

Luke's Side-By-Side Focus on the Exalted Jesus

Luke's Gospel in combination with the Book of Acts significantly enriches our understanding of how the two categories of Jesus' life and ministry dovetail. Many Bible scholars understand the two books as a kind of Part 1/Part 2 of the same overall work. Luke's introduction to the Book of Acts supports this view: "In the first book, O Theophilus, I have dealt with all that Jesus began to do and teach."[15] That's a reference to the historical Jesus, about whom Luke had already written extensively in his Gospel account, carefully investigating everything about Him from the beginning and then writing it down in an "orderly account."[16]

Back in the Book of Acts, Luke continues his opening: "until the day when he was taken up."[17] The words "taken up" refer to Jesus' Ascension, which elsewhere is closely linked to Jesus being seated at the right hand of the Father.[18] So the second part of Luke's introduction stands as a clear reference to the exalted Jesus.

It seems odd at first to find a reference to Jesus' exaltation so closely aligned to one focused on His humiliation. However, the theme of humiliation in association with the historical Jesus has always been juxtaposed with the realities of His subsequent exaltation. For instance, set alongside Jesus' statement, "everyone who exalts himself will be humbled," we find, "but the one who humbles himself will be exalted."[19] In the birth account, the appearance of the angels to the shepherds announcing Jesus' nativity foreshadows the glory that will belong to Jesus in His exaltation. In other words, the humiliation of the historical Jesus was always intended to be only part of the story. The rest of the story is the exalted Jesus in all His glory. The Apostle Paul summarizes this beautifully as he quotes from an early hymn of the Church:

"Who though he was in the form of God,
Did not count equality with God a thing to be grasped,
But made himself nothing, Taking the form of a servant,
Being born in the likeness of men. And being found in human form,
He humbled himself By becoming obedient to the point of death,
Even death on a cross! Therefore God has highly exalted him
And bestowed on him the name that is above every name,
So that at the name of Jesus every knee should bow,
In heaven and on earth and under the earth,
And every tongue confess that Jesus Christ is Lord,
To the glory of God the Father."

Philippians 2:5-11

This Same Jesus

The balance of what Luke wrote near the beginning of the Book of Acts adds significantly to our general understanding of both categories of who and what Jesus is. Luke refers to a kind of bridge between the two, recalling that Jesus was taken up "after he had given commands through the Holy Spirit to the apostles whom he had chosen."[20]

Luke also explains: "He presented himself alive to them after his suffering by many proofs, appearing to them during forty days and speaking about the kingdom of God."[21] The bridge between Jesus' humiliation and exaltation turns out to be a period of forty days following the resurrection. During this time, Jesus proved He had conquered death, and He connected the dots between His suffering and His role as Messiah in God's kingdom. On one occasion shortly after His death, Jesus met up with two grieving disciples who had heard about the empty tomb but did not know what to make of it. Jesus not only informed them of His resurrection, but He also gave them a lecture on all that the Jewish Scriptures taught about His suffering and ultimate entrance in glory.[22] On another occasion, Jesus made certain promises to the disciples, while indicating there would be a gap of time, of indefinite duration, between what would happen next and His eventual return "to restore the kingdom to Israel."[23]

Then Luke explains: "And when he had said these things, as they were looking on, he was lifted up, and a cloud took him out of their sight."[24] In other words, Jesus ascended to the right hand of the Father, marking the beginning of His exaltation as Lord.

The disciples were stunned. They stood staring into the sky, straining desperately to see Jesus even after He disappeared behind the clouds. Suddenly "two men in white robes" appeared standing beside them.[25] The men spoke, snapping the disciples out of their upward gaze: "Men of Galilee," they said, "why do you stand looking into heaven? This Jesus, who was taken up from you into heaven, will come in the same way as you saw him go into heaven."[26] In other words, just as the historical Jesus had ascended to the right hand of the Father to mark the beginning of His exaltation, so He would return one day to consummate His reign as Lord of lords.

Jesus would be the same when He returned, in that He would return bodily, bearing the marks of suffering and death by crucifixion, but doing so in glorious splendor. When He re-entered the physical world, He would be the same Jesus, but His impact would be totally different. In His first coming, He impacted the physical world only in part and only on occasion. At His return, He would thoroughly renew the physical world and He would reign in total victory.

The early disciples got the point. The historical Jesus had become the exalted Jesus. He had ascended "to the right hand of the power of God" and nothing could stop Him now. [27] Someday He would return in all of His glory.

How would you describe what happens at Jesus' return to an unbeliever? What might you say to them about Jesus' exaltation in relation to that event?

Describe how "waiting" for the Lord's return should impact a believer's life?

What is the significance of calling the hope of Jesus' return a "blessed hope" (Titus 1:13)?

How does the hope of Jesus' return impact your life personally on a day-to-day basis?

1 Or that there is something true of the one and fabricated of the other **2** John 16:28 **3** Luke 22:69. See also Hebrews 1:4-13. Jesus being "seated at the right hand of the power of God" indicates His exaltation, not just the Father's satisfaction with His payment for our sin. **4** Luke 1:46-48 **5** Leviticus 12:6-7 **6** Leviticus 12:8 **7** Luke 2:22-24 **8** Luke 18:14 **9** Philippians 2:5 **10** 1 Peter 5:6 **11** Luke 2:34-35 **12** Psalm 27:8 **13** Philippians 2:10-11 **14** Romans 10:9-10 **15** Acts 1:1 **16** Luke 1:3 **17** Acts 1:2 **18** See, for example, Hebrews 1:1-3 **19** Luke 18:14 **20** Acts 1:2 **21** Acts 1:3 **22** See Luke 24:13-35 **23** Acts 1:6 **24** Acts 1:9 **25** Acts 1:10 **26** Acts 1:11 **27** Luke 22:69

All that my heart deemed
   as true, now I realize
Was just a glimpse of the
   real You, my eternal prize
My heart, my mind, change it all
   from what I knew before
Forgive my making You so small,
   my exalted Lord

Lyrics from "Under Your Lordship"
by Amy Branson Fata

3

Hearts Burning Within Us

Shortly after the resurrection, certain disciples encountered Jesus on the road that leads to the village of Emmaus, about seven miles from Jerusalem.[1] The disciples did not recognize Jesus at first, though they soon experienced a profound "Aha! moment" as "beginning with Moses and all the Prophets, he interpreted to them in all the Scriptures the things concerning himself."[2] Once the eyes of the disciples "were opened" and they "recognized" Jesus, he "vanished from their sight."[3] Turning to one another, the overwhelmed disciples asked: "Did not our hearts burn within us while he talked to us on the road, while he opened to us the Scriptures?"[4]

"Hearts aflame"—how apt a description for the kind of response to the exalted Lord Jesus that arises from the inmost being of people who see and embrace Him for who He really is.

How else might you describe the intense thoughts and feelings of a person whose heart is burning because of encounters with Jesus?

According to Luke 24:13-35, what specific thing did Jesus do that resulted in the eyes of the disciples being opened? Why would that specific thing have had such an impact?

The Ideal "Man From Heaven"

Jesus pointed the Emmaus bound disciples to His exaltation with the question, "Was it not necessary that the Christ should suffer these things and enter into his glory?"[5] The entry into glory Jesus spoke of was His ascension to the right hand of the Father in heaven. Paul summarized the connection in his first letter to Timothy, quoting from an early Christian hymn in reference to Jesus:

> "He was manifested in the flesh,
> vindicated by the Spirit,
> seen by angels,
> proclaimed among the nations,
> believed on in the world,
> taken up in glory."
>
> 1 Timothy 3:16

No wonder the disciples could hardly contain themselves as they listened to the Scriptures about the Christ, the ideal person, the ideal "man from heaven"[6] and the one for whom all of history had been waiting ever since the Fall. As an exalted "king,"[7] He is the "royal son" endowed by God with "justice" and "righteousness", the one who will "judge with righteousness" and bless His subjects with "prosperity." His rule is as refreshing and renewing as "showers that water the earth." His land yields bumper crops of fruit and grain. His righteous subjects flourish and "abound."

He "defends the cause of the poor." He "crushes the oppressor." No one will prevail with violence over those whose blood is so "precious in His sight." The weak find pity in Him. The needy find life in Him. He hears when they cry and He delivers them.

His reign extends to the farthest regions of the earth. All nations receive blessings through Him and "call him blessed." People come from everywhere to worship and adore Him. Other lesser kings bring Him "tribute" and "gifts" of gold. They "fall down before Him" as everyone "serves" Him. They praise His wonderful name forever, as He fills the earth with His glory. He reigns from "sea to sea and from the River to the ends of the earth."

He is the exalted Lord and Christ! Everything about Him calls for a burning, heart-deep response of trust and loving appreciation!

Read Isaiah chapters 60-63. What similar descriptions of the king's person and rule do you find there? Make a list of at least 10 descriptions quoting what is written and referencing the specific chapter and verse:

1.

2.

3.

4.

5.

6.

7.

8.

9.

10.

Other Examples of Hearts Burning Within

Shortly after Jesus' entry into public ministry during the time of His humiliation, Andrew, the brother of Simon Peter, became one of the first to recognize Jesus for who He was and is. Following his initial encounter with Jesus, Andrew's burning heart sent him running to find his brother. "We have found the Messiah!" he declared.[8] So "he brought him to Jesus."[9]

A similar scene played out the next day in Galilee between Philip and his brother, Nathanael. "We have found him of whom Moses in the Law and also the prophets wrote, Jesus of Nazareth, the son of Joseph," Philip announced excitedly. "Come and see!"[10]

Refer to Mathew 8:18-22. What is the significance of Jesus not allowing some people to follow Him? Can you think of any other NT examples of Jesus turning someone away from following Him?

Use two or three sentences to tell the story of someone you know who gave up something significant to associate with Jesus.

Intrinsic Value and Bargains

Whenever the eyes of people were opened to see Jesus for who He is, the one described by Psalm 72 and by so many other Scriptures, their hearts began to burn within them. They began to treasure Jesus and the time they were able to spend in His presence. Many willingly left behind goods, occupation, and family simply for the privilege of associating with Jesus more closely.

Jesus once told a parable comparing the kingdom of heaven to a treasure hidden in a field and another to a pearl of great value.[11] In both cases, Jesus explained that once people understood the value of the treasures they found, they sold everything in order to become the owners. In other words, the people counted the cost and recognized a bargain when they saw one! They calculated the potential gain to far exceed whatever they had to pay to secure the treasure!

Bargains like the ones Jesus mentioned also form part of the Old Testament's teaching. For instance, the patriarch Jacob fell asleep one night on his way to Haran from Beersheba. As he slept, he dreamed of a stairway "set up on the earth, and the top of it reached to heaven."[12] He saw "the angels of God ascending and descending" on the stairway, with the Lord himself standing "above it."[13] The Lord promised in that moment to bless Jacob and his descendants, along with "all the families of the earth" through them.[14] Though he had been dreaming, Jacob quickly realized that the promise was real. The angels he had seen were just a glimpse of the activity of God directed toward its fulfillment.

When Jacob arose early the next morning, he excitedly marked the spot with a stone, believing he had found a treasure. He had discovered, so he thought, "the house of God" and "the gate of heaven."[15] Jacob believed he had found the place on earth where he could go to receive all the treasures of God's blessing, treasures very similar to the ones described in Psalm 72 and Matthew 13.

Once Jacob discovered his treasure, he too organized his life and resources to be near and preserve it. He moved his entire household to Bethel, making it the center of his worship and a symbol of God delivering him from Esau's anger. At Bethel, Jacob received confirmation of his new name, Israel, and of the promises God made to his father and grandfather before him, promises now to be fulfilled through him. In Jacob's heart, Bethel truly would always be treasured as "the house of God."[16]

How is Jacob's experience of wrestling with God (Genesis 32:22-31) similar to what happened at Bethel? What differences do you see?

Jesus and Nathanael

Jesus spoke of Jacob's treasure to Nathanael when Philip brought the two together. Nathanael had picked up on something unusual in what Jesus said to him by way of introduction: "Behold, an Israelite indeed, in whom there is no deceit!" and "Before Philip called you, when you were under the fig tree, I saw you."[17] When Nathanael processed the implications of Jesus seeing him beneath the fig tree and knowing the thoughts of his heart, he declared: "Rabbi, you are the Son of God! You are the King of Israel!"[18] Nathanael's words show his heart's assessment of Jesus as a wonderful treasure from God.

Jesus responded by saying: "Because I said to you, 'I saw you under the fig tree', do you believe? You will see greater things than these...you will see heaven opened, and the angels of God ascending and descending on the Son of Man."[19] Jesus wanted Nathanael to understand that his initial assessment of Jesus as a treasure from God was destined to be wonderfully fulfilled. The gateway into the heavens was not to be found in a place, but in a person. Jesus claimed to be that person, a treasure Himself and the one through whom all the other treasurers of God's activity to bless the earth become accessible.

Jesus is indeed The Treasure lying in the field, which any sensible person recognizes as valuable enough to be worth everything else he or she owns in exchange. He is The Pearl for which any merchant would be willing to pay the highest price for the privilege of becoming its owner. Jesus is the one for whom the hearts of men burn with excitement and zeal once He becomes theirs.

Identify at least three other persons or things that you might be tempted to make a treasure of your heart?

Relate a personal story of something extreme you have done in the past in order to possess an earthly treasure.

The Emmaus-bound Disciples

The disciples on the road to Emmaus eventually returned to Jerusalem, where "they found the eleven and those who were with them gathered together."[20] They told them everything that happened. Then Jesus Himself broke in, appeared in their midst, and gave an even more complete explanation: "Thus it is written, that the Christ should suffer and on the third day rise from the dead, and that repentance and forgiveness of sins should be proclaimed in his name to all nations, beginning from Jerusalem. You are witnesses of these things. And behold, I am sending the promise of my Father upon you. But stay in the city until you are clothed with power from on high."[21]

With that Jesus led them out to the vicinity of Bethany. After He blessed them, He "parted from them and was carried up into heaven."[22] Thus, the era of Jesus' exaltation began. Soon others would join His earliest followers in the "great joy" of discovering the dearest treasure of their hearts. [23]

*The hearts of people always respond favorably to what they treasure most.
Do you agree or disagree? Why or why not? Can you think of any specific
Scripture to support this statement?*

*What are the treasures of your heart? Describe what you do
to shower them with honor and attention? What is the most extreme
thing you have done to acquire an earthly treasure?*

*Read Matthew 6:19-21. How would you summarize the points
Jesus made about earthly treasures in these verses?*

1 Luke 24:13 **2** Luke 24:27 **3** Luke 24:31 **4** Luke 24:32 **5** Luke 24:26 **6** 1 Corinthians 15:47
7 The quoted words that follow in this and the next two paragraphs are found in Psalm 72:1-20.
8 John 1:41 **9** John 1:42 **10** Matthew 13:44-47 **11** Genesis 28:12. See Genesis 28:10-17 for the entire story.
12 Genesis 28:12-13 **13** Genesis 28:14 **14** Genesis 28:17 **15** Ibid. **16** Ibid. **17** John 1:47, 48 **18** John 1:49
19 John 1:50-51 **20** Luke 24:33 **21** Luke 1:46-49 **22** Luke 24:51 **23** Luke 24:52

4

DEFEAT OF HIS ENEMIES

All power's been given
   into His hand
Each hour, every minute,
   at His command
Reigning victorious,
   at the Father's side
Sin and death and unbelief,
   now crucified

Lyrics from "All Power"
by Amy Branson Fata

The apostles had plenty to talk about on their short walk back to Jerusalem after Jesus' ascension. Even if they ambled on in silence, they must have anticipated the lively discussion and time of corporate prayer sparked by their arrival in the "upstairs" room "where they were staying."[1] More than one hundred others would be counting on them to provide leadership as they waited patiently for Jesus to fulfill His promise of the Holy Spirit and power. To be sure, Jesus' ascension into "heaven" was not some kind of afterthought or epilogue to His suffering, death, and resurrection.[2] It was an intentional part of a much larger plan clearly identified in Scripture. Jesus ascended into heaven to assume His role as the exalted Lord. He would remain there "until the time for restoring all the things about which God spoke by the mouth of his holy prophets long ago". [3]

The Apostle Peter was the first to summarize the purpose of Jesus' exaltation, when on Pentecost he explained to the breathless crowd of Temple celebrants the sound they had heard of a "mighty rushing wind" coming from heaven. [4] Peter told them it was the exalted Lord Jesus "pouring out" the Holy Spirit, whom He had "received from the Father."[5] Peter also quoted King David from the Old Testament, asserting that David's words could not have been referring to anyone other than Jesus. After all, David "died and was buried, and his tomb is with us to this day."[6] Furthermore, David did not ascend to heaven, and yet he said, "The Lord said to my Lord, Sit at my right hand until I make your enemies your footstool."[7]

What images come to mind when you think of someone's enemies becoming a footstool?

What contrast might you draw between the fate of Jesus' enemies and the description of believers noted by the Apostle Paul in 2 Corinthians 2:14-16?

Footstools and Utter Defeat

Footstools are not positions of honor. It takes no special skill for someone to serve as a footstool for someone else. Just stand there, low to the ground, and hold up the feet of the person who is obviously far more important than you. In the case of Jesus' enemies, being made a footstool for His feet also signifies ultimate and utter defeat. Jesus' enemies might experience tactical victories now and then; but, in the end, they will be routed, totally dishonored, and reduced to nothing more than a lowly footstool for their Conqueror.

Numerous Scriptures call attention to the routing of Jesus' enemies as one of the chief purposes of His exaltation. Psalm 2 warns "the kings of the earth" to be "wise" in response to the Father's declared intent to install and exalt his King "on Zion, my holy hill."[8] The nations will be made the "heritage" and "possession" of this King, the Father's Anointed, who will "rule them with a rod of iron and dash them in pieces like a potter's vessel."[9]

In similar fashion, Hebrews 1 highlights God's "anointing" of the Son "beyond his companions."[10] It also echoes the prophecy of Psalm 110, underscoring the defeated position of Jesus' enemies as a "footstool" for His feet.[11] Meanwhile, Hebrews 2 draws from Psalm 8 to indicate that God has "put everything in subjection under his feet", leaving "nothing outside his control."[12] 1 Corinthians 15 adds that "the last enemy to be destroyed is death."[13]

Read Hebrews 1 and 2. Make a list of the references to Jesus' exaltation as Lord found in these two chapters. Note both the specific word or phrase used and the verse in which it is found.

Why does the writer of Hebrews go to such lengths to establish Jesus' position as the exalted Lord?

Enemies of the Exalted Lord

Besides death, sin and unbelief will also be brought under Jesus' feet. Sin, death, and unbelief are labels that summarize three major categories of Jesus' enemies. For example, the enemy of sin represents both the sin nature and the specific thoughts and acts that miss the mark of God's glory. The enemy of death includes such things as disease and deformity, along with injury and aging, not to mention all of the associated pain and suffering that go with each of these. The category of unbelief takes in doubt, fear, and even ignorance of the truth. Unbelief also stands for outright rejection of the truth about Jesus, whether related to His humiliation or to His exaltation as Lord.

Spiritual forces, both demonic and human, associate themselves with each of the three categories of Jesus' enemies. Therefore, when we speak of the enemies of Jesus, we also speak of the demonic and human champions of sin, death, and unbelief. During the time of Jesus' humiliation, demons often sought to bring about human suffering and death. They also championed episodes of sin and unbelief. Their most striking successes resulted in a member of Jesus' inner circle betraying Him and in Jesus' own people joining with the Romans to murder Him.

Human champions of sin, death, and unbelief at times can seem just as powerful as their demonic counterparts. Psalm 2 reveals that "kings and rulers of the earth" will be chief among those who stand in opposition to the exalted Lord.[14]

What other examples can you find in the Scriptures of demonic and human champions of...

Sin?

Death?

Unbelief?

What means do demonic and human champions of sin, death, and unbelief use today in opposition to the Lord? Share an illustration with your answer.

Unlimited Explosive Power

Demons, rulers, and kings are powerful enemies. Their abilities individually to champion sin, death, and unbelief can wreak large scale havoc. When acting in concert, their abilities become even more formidable. Defeating them is never child's play, but requires overwhelming, supra-human force. Fortunately, unlimited explosive power is a premier feature of Jesus' exaltation as Lord.

Following His arrest, Jesus stood before the chief priests and teachers of the law, who asked him: "If you are the Christ, tell us."[15] Jesus must have looked rather weak in that moment, having been blindfolded, mocked, and beaten by His guards prior to His appearance before the council. Jesus answered the chief priests and teachers with a clear declaration of His exalted position soon to be realized: "But from now on the Son of Man shall be seated at the right hand of the power of God."[16]

The term for "power" in the original language of the Bible is "dynamis", which is transliterated "dynamite." Dynamite is the perfect word for scientists to have employed as the name for the explosive crystalline compound known otherwise as TNT. "Dynamis" signifies an inherent and unlimited ability to act, an ability that can manifest itself spontaneously (i.e., explosively).

Upon His ascension, Jesus sat down at the right hand of the explosively powerful God, where He now possesses all the power necessary to utterly defeat His enemies, to make them His footstool, and to rule over them and everything else forever and ever. Someday, when Jesus returns, there will be a spontaneous display of His powerful wrath. Accordingly, Psalm 2 warns kings and rulers to be "wise" or responsive now, for the Lord's "wrath is quickly kindled."[17]

In the meantime, spontaneous (explosive) displays of the Lord's unlimited power against His enemies can break out at any moment. Jesus promised such to the apostles shortly before His ascension: "You will receive power when the Holy Spirit has come upon you."[18] Jesus began fulfilling this promise a few days later on the Day of Pentecost with an impressive victory over unbelief.

The promise of explosive power associated with Jesus' exaltation was not intended to guarantee an uninterrupted string of tactical victories prior to His return. Jesus' enemies are capable of winning tactical victories for now (although the Lord ultimately weaves even those into His larger and more strategic victory in the end). Jesus' promise also did not indicate that tactical victories would increase or pile up one on the other until the scales finally tip and victory becomes His. The promise of the Holy Spirit and power simply indicated that the age of Jesus' exaltation was about to begin and that it would begin with some spectacular displays of His explosive and unlimited ability to act. It would be the same caliber of explosive and unlimited ability that was displayed previously when He rose from the dead and that would be unleashed without limit again someday when He returns to make footstools of all His enemies.

What emphasis do the following verses place on power in the life and ministry of believers in Christ?

Romans 1:16

2 Corinthians 4:7

2 Corinthians 9:8 ("able" is "powerful")

2 Corinthians 12:9

Ephesians 1:18-21

Ephesians 3:14-21

Philippians 3:10

2 Timothy 1:7

2 Peter 1:3

Which verse or set of verses is especially meaningful to you? Why?

Surpassing Greatness

Knowing and understanding the purpose of Jesus' exaltation in terms of the defeat of His enemies provides additional insight into why someone like Paul walked away from all he previously held dear for "the surpassing worth of knowing Christ Jesus my Lord."[19] Paul was keenly aware that Jesus' enemies of sin, death, and unbelief, along with their human and demonic champions, had made this world a dangerous place to live. He knew he personally would have to avail himself of the explosive power of the exalted Lord in his own daily struggle, and so he made the all-consuming aim of his life "to know Christ and the power of his resurrection."[20]

Paul was not the first person to focus on knowing the unlimited, explosive power of the exalted Lord Jesus. When the apostles returned to the Upper Room in Jerusalem, there were about 120 men and women gathered there to hear their report on Jesus' ascension into the clouds and to join them in prayer as they waited for what was to come.[21]

Soon Peter "stood up among the brothers" and began directing the group toward choosing a replacement for Judas the betrayer.[22] Ultimately, "they cast lots for them, and the lot fell on Matthias, and he was numbered with the eleven apostles."[23]

A careful reader of Luke's narrative will note that before casting lots, the group prayed to the Lord (meaning Jesus), asking Him to "show which one of these two you have chosen to take the place in this ministry and apostleship."[24] The reason Luke bothers to include this part of the story is to underscore how the apostles expected the exalted Lord Jesus to rule powerfully among them from His position at the right hand of the power of God. The early believers were keenly aware that Jesus had sat down on a throne, not a Lazy-Boy. He would be ruling, not reclining.

Luke devotes more than half of Acts chapter one to the details of what happened immediately after Jesus' ascension into heaven. That the apostles returned to Jerusalem so quickly indicates the value they placed on obeying the exalted Lord.[25] As they waited, they took reasonable steps to organize and thus ready themselves for what lay ahead, the first spontaneous display of the exalted Lord's explosive and unlimited ability to act.

What percentage of your life as a believer do you live in conscious, active reliance on the Lord's power?

What might help you to grow in your reliance on the Lord's power?

What Scripture might you use as you answer these questions?

Identify an area of your life for which the power of Christ is needed?

What role does obedience and organization play in your experience of waiting on the Lord for His provision of power?

1 Acts 1:13 **2** Acts 1:11 **3** Acts 3:22 4 Acts 2:2 **5** Acts 2:33 **6** Acts 2:29 **7** Acts 2:34-35 **8** Psalm 2:2, 6, 10
9 Psalm 2:8, 2, 9 **10** Hebrews 1:9 **11** Psalm 110:1 **12** Hebrews 2:6-8; Psalm 8:6 **13** 1 Corinthians 15:26
14 Psalm 2:2 **15** Luke 22:67 **16** Luke 22:69 **17** Psalm 2:12 **18** Acts 1:8 **19** Philippians 3:8 **20** Philippians 3:10
21 Acts 1:14 **22** Acts 1:15 **23** Acts 1:26 **24** Acts 1:24-25 **25** Acts 1:4

Be gone unbelief,
  my Savior is near
And for my relief
  will surely appear
By prayer let me wrestle,
  He will perform
With Christ in the vessel,
  I smile at the storm
Be gone unbelief,
  and sin no longer reign
I count all things loss,
  knowing Christ is gain

Lyrics from "The Conqueror's Song"
by Amy Branson Fata

5

VICTORY OVER UNBELIEF

The enemy of unbelief holds remarkable sway over people everywhere as the default heart-response to the truth about Jesus, a reality suggested by Isaiah's question: "Who has believed what he has heard from us?"[1] In some nations, less than one-half of 1% of the population profess faith in the Lord Jesus, the rest either rejecting the good news outright or refusing to listen in the first place. Even among people where the gospel enjoys a more favorable rate of response, the power of unbelief still shows itself in the "hard" cases, validating comparisons to the difficulty of a camel passing through the eye of a needle.[2]

*What specific person or people group are you praying
for or encouraging to believe on the Lord?*

How would you describe the stronghold that unbelief has in the case of this person (these persons)?

Turn To Me and Be Saved

The believers who had assembled in the upper room shortly after Jesus sat down at the right hand of the Father waited there until the day of Pentecost. Pentecost marked the beginning of the summer wheat harvest, one of two harvests the people of Israel celebrated each year.[3] The first harvest occurred in the spring two days after the beginning of Passover, representing the first fruits of the crop planted the previous winter. Fifty days later, on Pentecost, a second harvest offering of "new grain" was presented to the Lord in the Temple in Jerusalem, along with burnt offerings of "seven lambs a year old without blemish, and one bull from the herd, and two rams."[4] The ceremony associated with this second harvest also included additional sacrifices of "one male goat for a sin offering and two male lambs, a year old, as a sacrifice of peace offerings."[5] Finally, on the day of Pentecost itself, the priest would also proclaim "a holy convocation," with mandatory attendance for all Jewish males, who were to come to Jerusalem from all their "dwelling places."[6]

These were the "devout men [Jews] from every nation under heaven" who "came together...and were bewildered" when they heard the sound of "a mighty rushing wind" blowing spontaneously "from heaven" and "filling the entire house" where the nearly 120 believers waited.[7] Earlier that day, they and all other Pentecost celebrants would have read publicly from Ezekiel, as they did year after year in their gatherings at the Temple.[8] Ezekiel is the prophet who gives the sad account of the departure of God's Shekinah Glory, first from the Temple and finally from the entire city of Jerusalem.[9] However, at the beginning of his prophecy, Ezekiel shares a marvelous report of the Lord's glory coming from out of the north, accompanied by wind and fire and voices.[10] As the celebrants read that day, no one would have blamed them for thinking that God's Shekinah Glory had returned to Jerusalem.[11] Strong winds did not blow in Jerusalem in early May, and the sight of "tongues as of fire" separating and coming to rest on the upstairs room would have only added to their speculations.[12]

Running to check things out, the crowd of worshippers discovered something entirely different from what they were expecting. They found the apostles "telling...the mighty works of God" in various languages and dialects, modeling the yet future fulfillment of God's plan for people from all the earth to respond with praise for the exalted Lord Jesus.[13] Jesus had been humiliated through crucifixion; He had been brutally murdered and then buried; but He also had been raised from the dead and exalted to the right of God. As a result, the words of Isaiah the prophet were beginning to come to pass:

> *"Turn to me and be saved, all the ends of the earth! For I am God, and there is no other. By myself I have sworn; from my mouth has gone out in righteousness a word that shall not return: To me every knee shall bow; every tongue shall swear allegiance. Only in the Lord, it will be said of me, are righteousness and strength; to him shall come and be ashamed all who were incensed against him"*[14]

What other verses can you think of that clearly indicate God's intent for people from every nation to hear of the Lord and His salvation? Select two and write them out in the space below:

According to Acts 2:4 and 17 respectively, to whom do Luke and Peter attribute the use of different languages among the apostles to "declare the wonders of God?"

What light do the following verses shed on this experience?

Acts 1:8

1 Corinthians 12:1-3

Responding With Amazement

At first, many in the crowd responded to what they saw and heard in "amazement."[15] The word amazement indicates a state of complete surprise, very colorfully illustrating how taken the people were. Caught off guard, they asked each another, "What does this mean?"[16]

There is nothing special about responding to Jesus (or to the truth about Him) with amazement. The Gospel accounts provide numerous illustrations of people who were amazed by Jesus and who marveled at all He did.[17] In the end, however, many of those same people eagerly joined in the chorus to crucify Him.

Amazement simply acknowledges that something unusual has caught a person's attention.

Unfortunately, amazement is as far as some people go with Jesus. They walk away from Jesus, saying: "Wow, did you see that! Did you hear that! Wasn't that something!" Yet they never go on to acknowledge and embrace Him by faith from the heart.

Read Luke 4:14-30. How did Jesus respond to the amazement of the people in the synagogue? What is the significance of his response? Can you think of any other occasions when he responded to someone's amazement?

Look up the following verses and then record the response directed toward Jesus' words or deeds:

Matthew 8:5-13

Matthew 8:18-20

Matthew 8:21-22

Matthew 8:23-27

Read Luke 8:1-18. Which type of soil corresponds best to a response of mere "amazement" at Jesus' words or deeds?

Rejection

On the day of Pentecost, the response of some in the crowd of worshippers moved beyond amazement to rejection. They "mocked" the apostles, saying: "They are filled with new wine."[18] Sometimes people mock what they don't understand. Sometimes they do understand, and their mocking is a form of calculated rejection. For example, when the Apostle Paul stood before the Areopagus in Athens proclaiming that God had "given assurance to all by raising him [Jesus] from the dead," they "mocked."[19] The members of the Areopagus had no trouble understanding what Paul proclaimed. They simply rejected it with derision.

The mockers on the day of Pentecost were loud enough and obnoxious enough to provoke a response from Peter. "These people are not drunk, as you suppose," he said. "It is only the third hour of the day."[20] The alcoholic wines available to most people were diluted with water. At nine in the morning, no one would have had sufficient time to consume enough wine to become drunk.

How does this account and Paul's experience on Mars prepare us for our own encounters with mockers?

What does 1 Peter 3:3-18 add to our understanding of mockers and how to respond to them?

Three Thousand Saved

After Peter boldly put the mockers in their place, he responded to others in the crowd who had indicated a more sincere desire to make sense out of what they had seen and heard. They asked: "Are not all these men who are speaking Galileans? How is it that we hear, each of us in his own native language? What does this mean?"[21]

To this group Peter advised, "give ear to my words."[22] Then he used a prophecy from Joel to explain what the crowd had seen and heard. As Joel predicted, when God poured out His Spirit on His servants, both men and women, they began to "prophesy."[23] In other words, they began to declare the praises and wonders of God. Furthermore, their declarations were accompanied by "signs and wonders;" such as the violent wind from heaven, the tongues of fire, and the apostles' use of languages they had not studied and did not know previously.[24] Indeed, the last days had begun, and eventually they would contain all of those things mentioned by Joel, including the sun being turned to darkness and the moon to blood. Within this period of time, however long it might be, the whole world would see "the great and magnificent day of the Lord", culminating in God's spectacular, once-for-all judgment on his enemies.[25] In the meantime, there now existed an open window of opportunity to repent and believe, for "everyone who calls upon the name of the Lord shall be saved."[26]

Peter then pointed the crowd to Jesus, saying that He was "attested by God with mighty works and wonders and signs that God did through him in your midst"; that God "delivered him up according to the definite plan and foreknowledge of God"; and finally that God "raised him from the dead and exalted him to his right hand."[27] For each of these assertions, Peter offered proof either from the Scriptures or from the testimony of eyewitnesses.

Halfway through the list of things God did, Peter leveled a stunning charge against his audience: "this Jesus...you crucified and killed by the hands of lawless men".[28] In other words, "You murdered Jesus!"

Peter offered no proof for his indictment. No proof was needed. The people knew they were guilty, and so "they were cut to the heart," prompting them to ask, "What shall we do?"[29] Peter told the people to "repent," meaning to change their minds about Jesus.[30] Previously they thought of Jesus as nothing more than a common insurrectionist. Now they knew the truth. Jesus is not a dead insurrectionist. He is the living and exalted Lord. Repenting of their old way of thinking would mean doing just as the prophet Joel had said: "calling on the name of the Lord to be saved."[31]

Peter also told the people to "be baptized, everyone of you, in the name of Jesus Christ for the forgiveness of your sins."[32] In other words, Peter asked those who did change their minds to give outward testimony of their new way of thinking (and believing) about Jesus as the exalted Lord. Consequently, Peter said they would "receive the gift of the Holy Spirit," as promised to both Jew and Gentile alike.[33]

Three thousand "received" Peter's message and "were baptized."[34] It was a mighty triumph of the exalted Lord over unbelief! Soon even more would join their ranks, for "the Lord added to their number day by day those who were being saved."[35] Each became a testimony to the power of the exalted Lord. Unbelief had initially closed their hearts to the truth about Jesus, but "the Lord opened" their hearts and they believed.[36]

Why should the conversions of the 3000 be considered a remarkable triumph over unbelief?

What relative, friend, co-worker, or acquaintance of yours would you consider to be a remarkable trophy of the Lord's power over unbelief if they were to profess faith in Jesus?

Read Ephesians 2:1-10. Why should every believer, including yourself, be considered a remarkable trophy of the Lord's power over unbelief?

Just Another Footstool

In the end, all unbelief will take its place under Jesus' feet with the rest of His enemies. Until then, even in some of the most unlikely places, and among some of the most unlikely people, we see example after example of the exalted Lord's power over unbelief whenever anyone professes heart-deep faith in Him. Encouraged by such displays during those early years, the apostle Paul wrote to the Colossians: "All over the world this gospel is bearing fruit and growing."[37] Paul's words still apply. The spontaneous and explosive ability of the exalted Lord to open hearts of unbelief continues today everywhere the Good News is proclaimed.

How do the conversion stories of Aeneas, Tabitha, and Cornelius from Acts 9 and 10 differ from the 3000 who were saved on the Day of Pentecost?

What types or categories of people do each of these represent as other potential trophies of the exalted Lord's power over unbelief?

What encouragement does the story in this lesson, along with verses such as Romans 1:16 and Colossians 1:6, offer us with regard to our duty to share the Gospel?

Share an example, either from your own conversion or an experience witnessing, of the exalted Lord's power over unbelief.

1 Isaiah 53:1 **2** Luke 18:23-25 **3** Acts 2:1 **4** Leviticus 23:16-18 **5** Leviticus 23:19 **6** Leviticus 23:21 **7** Acts 2:1-6
8 Howard, Kevin, and Marvin J. Rosenthal. The Feasts of the Lord. Orlando, FL: Zion's Hope, 1997. **9** Ezekiel 7-11
10 Howard and Rosenthal **11** Ezekiel 1:4ff **12** Acts 2:3 **13** Acts 2:11 **14** Isaiah 45:22-24 **15** Acts 2:7
16 Acts 2:12 **17** Luke 9:43 **18** Acts 2:13 **19** Acts 17:32-34 **20** Acts 2:15 **21** Acts 2:7-12 **22** Acts 2:14 **23** Acts 2:17
24 Acts 2:19 **25** Acts 2:20 **26** Acts 2:21 **27** Acts 2:22-33 **28** Acts 2:23 **29** Acts 2:37 **30** Acts 2:38 **31** Acts 2:21
32 Acts 2:38 **33** Acts 2:39 **34** Acts 2:41 **35** Acts 2:47 **36** Acts 16:13 **37** Colossians 1:6 (NIV)

Exalted, LORD

6

VICTORY OVER SIN

Save me from myself,
    for I am fallen
Cast my wicked ways
    into the sea
In the midst of darkness,
    You come callin'
Your light of truth
    shines over me

Savior, come, save
Healer, come, heal
Lord, come, reign
Save, heal, reign

Lyrics from "Save, Heal, Reign"
by Amy Branson Fata

The Apostle Paul could hardly believe what Barnabas, a trusted emissary from the church in Jerusalem, was telling him. Some of the persecuted believers from Jerusalem had found their way to Antioch. As they settled in, they "spoke to the Hellenists also, preaching the Lord Jesus."[1] Consequently, "a great number who believed turned to the Lord."[2]

Barnabas explained to Paul how the other apostles had sent him to Antioch when "the report of this came to the ears of the church in Jerusalem."[3] Upon arriving, Barnabas saw for himself how God was blessing, so he gladly joined in. His obvious faith, character, and empowerment from the Spirit gave him instant credibility as a godly leader. Soon "a great many people were added to the Lord," which is why Barnabas had sought Paul's help.[4] Barnabas could think of no better person to teach these new "Christians" than Paul, the one Jesus himself commissioned "to carry his name before the Gentiles."[5]

What Paul found when he arrived in Antioch signaled nothing less than a profound victory of the exalted Lord over unbelief among Gentiles. Paul also discovered an equally profound victory over sin. The Lord's victory over sin among the believers in Antioch serves as a tribute to His explosive power to transform the lives of everyone who believe on Him.

Why was Barnabas perfectly suited for the role he played as an emissary to Antioch? See Acts 5:36-37; 9:26-27; 1 Cor. 9:6.

Take a moment to reflect on how your life has changed since you became a believer in Christ. How would you describe your own personal transformation?

Sin's Reign in Antioch

The darkness of sin ruled powerfully in Antioch prior to the arrival of the persecuted believers from Jerusalem. The Roman Emperor Julian described the city as "gay and prosperous."[6] So cosmopolitan were Antioch's citizens, one of their own boasted:

"If a man had the idea of traveling all over the earth with a concern not to see how the cities looked but to learn their ways, Antioch would fulfill his purpose and save him journeying. If he sits in our market-place, he will sample every city; there will be so many people from each place with whom he can talk."[7]

Antioch was founded by a Macedonian general named Seleukos. Legend has it that Seleukos was offering an animal sacrifice to Zeus one day, when suddenly an eagle swooped down, bit into the sacred meat, and flew away toward Mount Silpios. Since eagles were known as "Zeus' bird," Seleukos and his men believed they had received a sign from the gods. They followed the eagle until it landed in the valley near Silpios and stood on the meat it had snatched from the altar.

The General and his men concluded that Zeus had led them to build a new city on the spot where the eagle stood. After laying its foundations, Seleukos called the new city "Antioch" after the name of his son. On the same day, Seleukos sacrificed a virgin, whom he later declared to be Antioch's Tyche or goddess of good fortune. The General then fashioned a statue in her likeness and placed it strategically inside the city.[8]

By the time Barnabas and Paul began ministering in Antioch more than three hundred years later, worship of the city's Tyche was in full swing. A temple had been built in honor of the goddess, with her statue standing in the temple's most sacred part. Roman coins depict the Tyche facing outward from the temple toward an altar, watching over the daily sacrifices offered as part of various sacred rituals.[9]

Unfortunately, the Tyche was not the only idol in Antioch. The other gods and goddesses of pagan Rome were there also and were worshipped just as fervently. Chief among them was the Emperor. The imperial cult of emperor worship made great headway into cities like Antioch due to its connection to Roman citizenship. Though everyone living in the empire was considered a subject, Roman citizenship "became a prize eagerly sought by conquered individuals who wanted a greater degree of security and rights under the law."[10]

Antioch was so steeped in worship of the Tyche, the Emperor, and a host of other gods and goddesses, that few other places on earth would have been more desperate for "the good news about the Lord Jesus."[11] The pervasive idolatry led to lifestyles chocked full of superstition and other pagan practices.

It also resulted in lifestyles of extravagant sensuousness. The nearby suburb of Daphne, named after a nymph once pursued by Apollo, became a kind of retreat center for licentiousness. By the time Paul and Barnabas came to Antioch, the people who lived there had become known as purveyors of "Daphne morals."

Read Acts 17-19. What references to idolatry, immorality, and paganism in the cities of Thessalonica, Berea, Athens, Corinth, and Ephesus do you find?

Turning to the Lord from Sin

Paul and Barnabas, along with the others who had fled from Jerusalem, saw "a great number" of people with Daphne morals "turn" in faith to the exalted Lord Jesus.[12] As the Lord began to triumph over sin in their lives, a completely different epithet began to attach itself to them. They became known as "Christians," meaning "little Christs."[13]

This change in the new believers in Antioch illustrates several dynamics related to the defeat of sin as an enemy of the exalted Lord Jesus. The enemy of sin is long entrenched on this earth and is capable of holding sway over entire cities, as it did in Antioch, or over entire civilizations, as it did throughout the Roman empire. The Apostle Paul traced the origin of sin to one man; namely, Adam, who ate of the forbidden fruit in the Garden of Eden. This act of disobedience, which we call original sin, Paul refers to simply as "the sin."[14]

The sin produced consequences far beyond what Adam could have ever imagined. One of them is the involvement of each of Adam's descendants in the sin. When Adam sinned, so did everyone else in the human race. In this way, everyone became subject to sin, along with unbelief and death. The human body in its fallen state became a kind of dwelling place for sin, something Paul referred to when he told the Romans: "the sin dwells in us."[15]

The sin thrives on the use of our bodies and minds to accomplish its ends of unbelief and death. In effect, our bodies and minds naturally serve as "instruments of the sin;" that is, as unholy tools of its unholy lordship.[16] When the sin is in charge, it is capable of manifesting itself in choices and behavior marked by such things as idolatry and Daphne morals. However, once people believe in their hearts on Jesus, they, with Jesus, "die to the sin."[17] They are freed from the sin's unholy lordship, enabling them instead to surrender their bodies and minds as instruments of righteousness under the exalted Lord Jesus. This enablement, which is instantaneous at the moment of conversion, launches a process of sanctification that continues over a lifetime.

Look up the word "sanctification" in a Bible dictionary. Write the definition below. Describe your personal experience with God's work of sanctification.

What biblical evidence is there to indicate that everyone has been impacted by original sin?

What specifically does Paul tell believers to "know", to "count", and to "offer" in Romans 6? What practical steps might someone take to put this strategy into practice?

Powerful Spiritual Forces

Daily encounters with the sin are encounters with powerful spiritual forces. In the city of Ephesus, for example, located near Antioch, the sin dominated people religiously, economically, and politically. Ephesus was known for its devotion to Artemis, an idol represented as a virgin-huntress. Legend had it that a statue of Artemis once fell from the sky onto the city of Ephesus. The people built a temple on the place where it fell and dedicated it to Artemis. Four times larger than the Parthenon, the temple featured 127 sixty-foot tall columns.

Shortly after Paul's arrival in Ephesus, tradesmen and other citizens began to see evidence of the exalted Lord gaining victory over unbelief and sin: "About that time there arose no little disturbance concerning the Way".[18] An idol maker by the name of Demetrius stirred up the people with pronouncements of "danger not only that this trade of ours may come into disrepute but also that the temple of the great goddess Artemis may be counted as nothing, and that she may even be deposed from her magnificence, she whom all Asia and the world worship."[19]

Hearing this, the people "were enraged."[20] For over two hours, thousands chanted repeatedly: "Great is Artemis of the Ephesians!"[21] The uproar did not quiet down until the city clerk was finally able to reason with the mob and dismiss them. In the meantime, the power of the spiritual forces aligned against the Lord and His people was on full display in response to so many in the city beginning to hold the name of the Lord in such "high honor."[22]

*What is the most severe form of opposition to the Gospel
you have ever faced? How did you deal with it?*

*Some Christians respond to opposition to their faith with self-censorship.
How would you advise another believer to overcome the temptation of self-
censorship when the Gospel message seems unpopular or unwelcome?*

Day-to-day Victory

Throughout his letters to various churches, the Apostle Paul
provides significant insight into how victory over the sin comes to us
through the power of the exalted Lord. For example, Paul wrote to the
Romans:

"If you confess with your mouth that Jesus is Lord and believe
in your heart that God has raised him from the dead, you will be
saved."[23]

A person's mouth is just one part of the body that by nature is
under the control of the enemy of sin. Sin is in control because of its
lordship over the heart. As it turns out, individual parts of a person's
body function as resources of that person's heart, resources that
express what is in the heart and that do the heart's bidding. When
people believe on Jesus in their heart, their believing heart will find
a way to express itself by means of the "instruments" at its disposal,
instruments which had formerly been under the power of unbelief
and sin. In other words, the parts of the body that once were under
the control of unbelief and sin now become available to the exalted
Lord to confess Him.

The day-to-day process that results in such victories is not without setbacks. Thankfully, daily victory over the enemies of unbelief and sin do not depend on our own power, but rather on the power of the exalted Lord, the same power whereby Jesus rose from the dead and which He shares with us freely. The Apostle Paul amplified this point to the Corinthians:

"No one who is speaking in the Spirit of God ever says, 'Jesus is accursed' and no one can say, 'Jesus is Lord,' except in the Holy Spirit."[24]

In other words, victories over unbelief and sin, victories that result in a person turning by faith to the Lord initially and then continuing to live as "a little Christ," depend on the empowering ministry of the Holy Spirit. With the Spirit's help, it is possible for believers to confess "Jesus is Lord" with everything they are and have.

Final and complete victory over the enemy of sin, like victory over the other enemies of the exalted Lord, does not come until the end, when it will be forced to become a lowly footstool. Until then, regardless of how formidable the enemy of sin might appear to be, we know the exalted Lord Jesus possesses the power to finish the job. As the Apostle Paul promised: "Being confident of this very thing, that he who has begun a good work in you will complete it until the day of Jesus Christ."[25]

What are some of the victories over sin you personally have experienced as a "little Christ"?

Make a list of at least ten "resources" of your heart. Be sure to include ones that lie outside of your body, but which are still within the command and control of your heart.

Which are you now using to confess "Jesus is Lord"?

What steps might you take to experience even more victory through the Spirit's empowerment?

1 Acts 11:20 **2** Acts 11:21 **3** Acts 11:22 **4** Acts 11:24 **5** Acts 11:26 and 9:15 **6** Kondoleon, Christine. Antioch: The Lost Ancient City. Princeton, NJ, University Press, 2000, 9. **7** Ibid, 11. **8** Ibid. **9** Ibid. **10** Ibid., 17. **11** Acts 11:20 (NIV) **12** Acts 11:21 **13** Acts 11:26: **14** Romans 5:12. The definite article "the" appears before the word "sin" in the original language of the New Testament **15** Romans 7:20 **16** Romans 6:11-13 **17** Romans 6:1-14 **18** Acts 19:23 **19** Acts 19:27 **20** Acts 19:28 **21** Ibid. **22** Acts 19:17-20 (NIV) **23** Romans 10:9-10 **24** 1 Corinthians 12:3 **25** Philippians 1:6 (NKJV)

To the brokenhearted,
  You are near
And in Your presence
  I will not fear
If I will call out to You
  with praise on my tongue
Then in my heart
  the battle's already won

There is a purpose to this pain
  My suffering is not in vain
There is eternal meaning
  to my despair
Though it may seem more
  than I can bear

Lyrics from "To the Brokenhearted"
by Amy Branson Fata

7

VICTORY OVER DEATH

Confusion raced through Peter's mind as he reflected on the events of the last few days. He was sitting in jail for the second time because of the "many signs and wonders" he and the other apostles had performed.[1] The miracles had resulted in those who were "sick" and "afflicted by unclean spirits" being relieved of their suffering.[2] But in spite of these victories, all suffering did not go away, not by a long shot. The chains on Peter's wrists and feet imposed on him their own significant measure of pain.

The cold darkness only added to the discomfort of Peter and the other apostles. Peter took heart, nevertheless, since they likely would not remain in their chains for long. The last time he and John had been thrown into jail it was only for one night. The rulers, elders, and teachers of the law let them go the following day with nothing more than a stern lecture "not to speak or teach at all in the name of Jesus."[3]

Peter and the others did get out of jail more quickly than they imagined. They were released miraculously "during the night [when] an angel of the Lord opened the doors of the jail and brought them out."4 But as joyful as their release was; once again, it still did not signal the end of their suffering at the hands of the authorities.

The next morning, Peter and the others returned to the temple courts "at daybreak and began to teach," as the angel had instructed them.5 The authorities eventually caught up to them, though they failed to solve the mystery of their escape. Taking the apostles back into custody, the authorities gave them another stern lecture. Then they "beat" them and let them go.6

According to Acts 5:41, why did the apostles go away from the Sanhedrin "rejoicing" after they were flogged?

What is so honorable about suffering for the Name of the Lord?

Describe some episode of your own personal suffering because of the Name of the Lord? What strategies did you employ to not give up or give in?

A Great Wave of Persecution

First there was jail, then flogging, with even more pain and suffering on the way. Stephen, who was doing "great wonders and signs among the people," was "seized" by the elders and teachers of the law and brought before the Sanhedrin.[7] Falsely charged with speaking against Moses and the Temple, the people "cast him out of the city and stoned him."[8] As a result, Stephen "fell asleep."[9]

Stephen's murder unleashed a "great" wave of persecution against the church at Jerusalem.[10] Many were "dragged away from their homes" and "committed to prison," with precious few of them ever experiencing the relief of a miraculous escape.[11] Most died instead. Far from being defeated by the exalted Lord Jesus, death seemed to be gaining the upper hand.

Pain and suffering and disease are all subsets of the category of Jesus' enemies we call death. Suffering itself takes on many forms, often beginning with the physical, and moving on to the emotional or psychological. When episodes of suffering descend on us, we often are left asking questions such as, How long is this going to last? Why is this happening to me? Does Jesus know? Does He care? Frailty, weakness, worthlessness, bewilderment, and soul-deep questions—these are the things we have come to expect and dread from death and its minions.

How would you describe the role that Scripture reading and meditation play in relieving suffering?

Share three favorite verses or passages you turn to for relief from pain and suffering?

Why do you think Psalm 23 is such a favorite for so many people in reference to death and suffering?

The Exalted Lord In Control

Death is the last enemy to be destroyed and made a footstool of the exalted Lord.[12] This does not mean death has free reign until then to do as it pleases. To the contrary, death and its cohorts of pain and suffering are subject to our exalted Lord even now. They may be able to wreak a lot of havoc, but they do not win in the end. They are like the demons during Jesus' time on earth that convulsed and shrieked when they were commanded to depart from some poor tormented person. They went out with their tails between their legs, their shrieks and paroxysms indicating defeat, not victory. Similarly today, under the Lordship of Jesus, the pain, suffering, and realities of death can be devastatingly harsh, but they are only the shrieks and paroxysms of defeated foes on the way to lowly places as footstools for the exalted Lord.

In the early days of Jesus' exaltation as Lord, Peter and the others experienced many different kinds of victories over pain and suffering and death, including episodes of complete healing and resurrection. They also experienced episodes of other less recognized types of victory. These become more clear as the various stories of suffering are juxtaposed.

For example, the story of the apostles getting flogged after spending a night in jail, when contrasted with the earlier story of their simply being jailed and released, seems to emphasize the growing intensity of persecution, with all of its attendant pain, suffering, and death.[13] However, when juxtaposed against later stories, such as the account of the murder of Stephen, or even that of the Apostle's Paul's conversion, other themes emerge.[14]

The murder of Stephen removed all doubt about the real endgame of the Lord's enemies. They were determined to squelch any mention of Jesus' name or demonstration of His power, even if it meant the use of violence and brutality. Stephen's accusers tried arguing at first, but "they could not withstand the wisdom and the Spirit with which he was speaking."[15] They resorted next to false accusations, but Stephen gave an impeccable defense followed by yet another witness to the reality of Jesus' exaltation and His "standing at the right hand of God."[16] Finally, when they could not drown out Stephen's testimony by "stopping their ears and crying out with loud voices," they murdered him.[17]

The other apostles could have met with a similar fate when they were taken into custody after their miraculous escape from jail in Acts 5. The high priest and Sanhedrin "were enraged and wanted to kill them."[18] So what stopped them? Why did they not inflict on the apostles the same violent and brutal death they later inflicted on Stephen? Because in the nick of time, Gamaliel, "a teacher of the law held in honor by all the people" argued persuasively against it, and they "took his advice."[19]

Setting all three stories side by side (the apostles' first imprisonment, their second imprisonment, and the murder of Stephen) clearly demonstrates the power of the exalted Lord Jesus to limit and control suffering. He is able to send angels to release His witnesses from prison unscathed. He is able to prevent their murder simply by turning the hearts of authorities toward some more lenient punishment. With His power to limit and control suffering so clearly established, only one conclusion is possible: the amount of suffering one experiences under Jesus' Lordship is what the Lord Jesus Himself allows. And if He is allowing it, there must be a purpose. And if there is a purpose, the suffering is filled with meaning. Thus, the exalted Lord Jesus triumphs over pain and suffering and death by controlling them, limiting them, and filling them with meaning for His glorious ends.

What do the following verses indicate about the possible meanings of pain and suffering?

John 16:21-22

Luke 8:13

Romans 5:1-4

James 1:2-8

2 Corinthians 12:7-10

Purpose and Meaning

The association of purpose and meaning with the Lord's control over suffering takes center stage in the story of Paul's conversion. The Damascus-bound persecutor of "those who belonged to the Way" encountered the exalted Lord in "a light from heaven, brighter than the sun, that shone" around him and those who traveled with him.[20] Immediately, Paul fell to the ground. When he stood up, he "opened his eyes", but "could see nothing."[21]

The blindness Paul suffered lasted only three days. The Lord instructed Ananias, a disciple who lived in Damascus, to go to Paul "and lay his hands on him so that he might regain his sight."[22] When Ananias obeyed, "something like scales fell from Paul's eyes, and he regained his sight."[23] It was the end of Paul's blindness, but not the end of his suffering as a witness for the exalted Lord. By his own account, Paul became subject to an unusual amount of suffering:

> "Are they servants of Christ? I am a better one...with far greater labors, far more imprisonments, with countless beatings, and often near death. Five times I received at the hands of the Jews the forty lashes less one. Three times I was beaten with rods. Once I was stoned. Three times I was shipwrecked; a night and a day I was adrift at sea; on frequent journeys, in danger from rivers, danger from robbers, danger from my own countrymen, danger from Gentiles, danger in the city, danger in the wilderness, danger at sea, danger from false brothers; in toil and hardship, through many a sleepless night, in hunger and thirst, often without food, in cold and exposure. And, apart from other things, there is the daily pressure on me of my anxiety for all the churches."[24]

None of the suffering Paul experienced spun out of the exalted Lord's control, nor did it take the Lord by surprise. In the instructions Jesus gave to Ananias, He explained that Paul was His "chosen instrument," saying: "I will show him how much he must suffer for the sake of my name."[25]

Jesus' words spell out with the greatest clarity the significant role He Himself plays in controlling and limiting the suffering of His witnesses. He personally knows both the "what" and "how much" of their suffering. And He knows it in advance, indicating that He is allowing it to happen. In other words, the exalted Lord Jesus has the power, not just to respond to suffering once it begins, but also to prevent it from ever getting started if He so chooses. Finally, the Lord leaves no doubt that He has a purpose for Paul's suffering. "He must suffer," the Lord told Ananias, "for the sake of my name."[26] Paul's initial blindness, coupled with all the other suffering he experienced, would somehow bless the name of Jesus, the one who had suffered so much for him.

Paul must have drawn encouragement from knowing that his suffering would be so meaningful. Suffering that is meaningful, suffering for which there is a known glorious purpose, is always easier to endure. However, the meaning of Paul's suffering would not be the only source of encouragement to Paul or, for that matter, to anyone else who suffers for the name of Jesus. Behind all of the emphasis on the exalted Lord's control of suffering lies the even more encouraging reality that Jesus cares about what happens to His people. Like a mother whose heart is pierced by some harm inflicted on her child, so the exalted Lord identifies and empathizes with the suffering of His people. This was the first lesson Jesus taught Paul when He confronted him with the reality of His resurrection and exaltation. The exalted Lord asked: "Saul, Saul, why are you persecuting me?"[27] Jesus' reference to Himself as the object of Paul's persecutions reveals His divine empathy with the sufferings of His people.

In the end, the exalted Lord Jesus sealed the doom of death and its minions when He rose again and sat down at the Father's right hand. As He orchestrates the events of His ultimate victory, He so graciously grants a variety of tactical triumphs here and now over death, disease, pain, and suffering. The tactical victories sometimes involve healing or other types of divine reversals, but they always involve controlling and limiting our suffering. Moreover, in them, the exalted Lord gives meaning and assures us of His care.

What other biblical examples are there of men and women of God who endured suffering? How did the Lord communicate to them or through them that He cared and was in control?

Other than Jesus, can you think of any examples historically of the Lord gaining victory through the death of one of his own?

How would you answer someone who questions whether the Lord cares about his or her suffering?

1 Acts 5:12 **2** Acts 5:16 **3** Acts 4:18 **4** Acts 5:19 **5** Acts 5:21 **6** Acts 5:40 **7** Acts 6:8 **8** Acts 7:58 **9** Acts 7:58-60 **10** Acts 8:1 **11** Acts 8:3 **12** 1 Corinthians 15:26 **13** See Acts 5 compared to Acts 3-4 **14** See Acts 6-7 compared to Acts 9 **15** Acts 6:10 **16** Acts 7:56 **17** Acts 7:57 **18** Acts 5:33 **19** Acts 5:34,40 **20** Acts 9:2; 26:13 **21** Acts 9:8 (NIV) **22** Acts 9:11-12 **23** Acts 9:18 **24** 2 Corinthians 11:23-28 **25** Acts 9:15-16 **26** Acts 9:16 **27** Acts 9:4

LORD
Exalted

8

PRESENT AMONG US

Jesus often spoke to His followers about how He would relate to them during the time of His exaltation. Being seated at the right hand of the Father meant He would be "going" to a place where they "cannot follow" for now.[1] The thought of no longer living with Jesus as they had from the beginning unsettled the disciples, provoking protests and resistance every time He mentioned it. Jesus compassionately coupled announcements of His impending departure with promises of His return and of His ever-presence in the meantime. One such promise stood out so prominently to Matthew, a member of the Twelve, he used it to close his gospel, quoting Jesus with these dramatic and powerful words: "And behold, I am with you always, to the end of the age."[2]

What other promises of Jesus' ever-presence can you recall from the New Testament?

What does it mean to you to know that Jesus is "with you"?

The Lord's Ever-presence and Personal Involvement

Jesus' promises to be ever-present with His disciples were especially comforting in light of the persecutions certain to follow His going. The disciples would be "delivered to synagogues and prisons," and made to stand before various earthly authorities, all "for my name's sake."[3] Nevertheless, Jesus would be fully aware of the threats and challenges. He pledged to personally provide the assistance, power, and other necessary resources to escape or endure, saying:

"Settle it therefore in your minds not to meditate beforehand how to answer, for I will give you a mouth and wisdom, which none of your adversaries will be able to withstand or contradict."[4]

In Acts, Luke illustrates how Jesus follows through on this promise on behalf of Stephen. Certain men "rose up and disputed with Stephen, but they could not withstand the wisdom and the Spirit with which he was speaking."[5]

In addition to His ever-presence with believers, the Book of Acts also contains numerous other examples of the exalted Lord Jesus personally orchestrating the defeat of His enemies. He is portrayed as taking an active role at the right hand of the Father; involved, for example, in "opening hearts," as He did with Lydia and Paul.[6]

Following Paul's conversion, Jesus continued to engage His new convert personally and with His ever-presence. One night in Corinth, the Lord spoke to Paul "in a vision." saying: "Do not be afraid, but go on speaking and do not be silent, for I am with you, and no one will attack you to harm you, for I have many people in this city who are my people."[7] So Jesus was personally "with" Paul in Corinth, not only to encourage him, but also to preserve his witness for the sake of bringing others to Himself.

The ever-presence and personal involvement of the Lord Jesus in power orchestrating the defeat of His enemies turns out to be a constant theme of the early years of His exaltation. The Book of Acts emphasizes Jesus making His power and presence known through a variety of means. Chief among them is the Holy Spirit working in the apostles, a reality that factors heavily into the story of Ananias and Sapphira.[8] The Lord also made His power and ever-presence known in those early years through dreams, visions, angels, and un-embodied voice, all of which were used similarly in the Old Testament to represent the presence and power of Jehovah.[9]

How did the Lord make His ever-presence and power known (a) in the choice of a replacement for Judas in Acts 1:12-16; and (b) in the result of the prayer meeting in Acts 4:23-31?

List examples from the Old Testament of Jehovah's ever-presence and power being represented similarly?

The Angel of the Lord

Another way the Lord manifested His ever-presence during the early years of His exaltation was through "the angel of the Lord." In the Old Testament, the angel of the Lord is widely recognized as representing the presence of Jehovah. Similarly, the angel of the Lord represents the Lord Jesus powerfully orchestrating the defeat of His enemies. For example, "an angel of the Lord" appeared to Peter in prison, taking him by the hand and "rescuing" him from Herod's clutches.[10]

Herod, the Governor of Judea, had mounted a challenge to the exalted Lord by executing James while taking Peter and others into custody. Peter's miraculous release frustrated Herod, but it did not stop him from continuing his challenge to "the word" about Jesus and His exaltation.

Herod "delivered an oration" to the people of Tyre and Sidon in response to their request for peace.[11] The people liked what they heard, so they shouted, "The voice of a god, and not of a man!"[12] Herod pompously allowed the undeserved accolade to stand, basking in the power of his will and word as an earthly king. With James dead, with Peter in hiding, and now with the enthusiastic praise of the people, it seemed obvious to Herod that his will and his word had prevailed. But Herod's glory was short lived, since "immediately an angel of the Lord struck him down."[13] Having fallen ill in this fashion, he was eventually "eaten by worms and breathed his last."[14] Herod became just another footstool for the exalted Lord Jesus, but "the word of God (that is, the message about Jesus) increased and multiplied."[15]

List other mentions of "the word of God" in the Book of Acts, noting how they too point to the ever-presence, power, and personal involvement of the exalted Lord in orchestrating the defeat of His enemies.

What examples from recent history can you give of the power of the message about Jesus over the attempts of men to destroy it or to silence the ones who proclaim it?

According to Matthew 5:11, what resources are available to those who are persecuted? What does this mean when the word itself is under attack?

An Angel of God and Cornelius

In a separate appearance of "an angel of God," a Roman "centurion" by the name of Cornelius was instructed to send for Peter, who was "lodging with one Simon, a tanner, whose house is by the sea."[16] At about the same time, the Lord personally spoke to Peter in a vision, telling him to kill and eat certain ceremonially unclean animals as a way of preparing him for the ministry of evangelizing Cornelius, a Gentile. So by means of the angel, as well as His own voice, the exalted Lord Jesus spoke to both men in separate places at about the same time. He also coordinated their encounter with each other so that Cornelius might hear "a message by which he and all his household would be saved."[17] In this manner, the exalted Lord Jesus personally orchestrated the beginning of the defeat of unbelief among the Gentiles.

What correlation do you see between Matthew 16:13-20
and the story of Peter and Cornelius?
Describe the role that Jesus played in both accounts.

What personal illustration can you give of the exalted Lord "coordinating"
your encounter with someone else for the sake of the Gospel?

The Name of Jesus

Yet another way in which the ever-presence and power of the exalted Lord is represented among his followers involves the use of Jesus' name. "Calling on the name of the Lord" is a practice that hearkens back to the Old Testament. In reference to Jesus, calling on the name of the Lord assumes certain realities that must be embraced by faith. The first is that Jesus rose from the dead and is alive. Calling on His name also means believing that God the Father exalted Him at His right hand. It also embraces the proposition that Jesus is able hear and willing to come and be present when His name is invoked. Finally, calling on the name of the exalted Lord also indicates faith that He will respond with the power associated with His exaltation. In this fashion, the name of the Lord came to serve as a premier way of referring to His ever-presence as the exalted Lord and personal involvement in the defeat of His enemies.

Soon after Jesus' exaltation, Peter and John called on His name to invoke His presence and power to heal the man who was "laid daily at the gate of the temple that is called the Beautiful Gate to ask alms of those entering the temple."[18] When the man asked for money, Peter told him: "I have no silver and gold, but what I do have I give to you. In the name of Jesus Christ of Nazareth, rise up and walk."[19] Immediately, the beggar's "feet and ankles were made strong. And leaping up, he stood and began to walk."[20]

The healing created quite a stir, eventually landing Peter and John before "the rulers, elders, and scribes in Jerusalem."[21] They asked Peter and John: "By what power or by what name did you do this?"[22] There is nothing surprising about this question, including the assumption that Peter and John had invoked a power of some kind to perform the healing. It was a commonly held superstition that some people were able to invoke the presence of powerful spiritual forces through incantations. If the invoker knew the name of the spiritual power, all the better. By calling on that name, the person could control or manipulate the power behind it.

The name of the Lord Jesus could not be used so profanely, not being subject to the whims and power grabs of unholy enchanters. The "seven sons of Sceva, a Jewish chief priest", found this out the hard way.[23] Having seen the power at work in the extraordinary miracles God did through Paul, the seven sons of Sceva "undertook to invoke the name of the Lord Jesus over those who had evil spirits", crying: "I adjure you by the Jesus, whom Paul proclaims" to come out.[24]

But the demon answered back: "Jesus I know, and Paul I recognize, but who are you?"[25] The demon then proceeded to jump on them and "overpowered them, so that they fled out of that house naked and wounded."[26] When this became known later, "fear fell upon them all, and the name of the Lord Jesus was extolled."[27]

The name of the Lord Jesus is to be treated with honor because of all His name signifies. The name of the Lord stands for the account of His life on earth as "the Holy and Righteous One" promised by God, the One executed unjustly on the cross, raised from the dead, and then taken to heaven, where He will remain "until the time for restoring all things about which God spoke by the mouth of his holy prophets long ago."[28] In other words, the name of the Lord stands for all He is from eternity past and on into the hereafter. This includes the declaration of His triumph over death, the reality that He is alive and well, exalted at the right hand of the mighty God. Therefore, the invocation of His name by faith pays tribute both to His presence and power as the exalted Lord. No wonder Peter did not hesitate to answer the rulers and elders with these words:

"If we are being examined today concerning a good deed done to a crippled man, by what means this man has been healed, let it be known to all of you and to all the people of Israel that by the name of Jesus Christ of Nazareth, whom you crucified, whom God raised from the dead—by him this man is standing before you well."[29]

What does it mean when a believer today says or does something "in Jesus' Name"?

What other Bible verses can you think of that tell believers something to do in the Name of Jesus?

Today the ever-presence and power of the Lord in His exaltation continues to play a prominent role in the life of believers as Jesus continues to orchestrate the ultimate defeat of His enemies. The exalted Lord Jesus is still present with us in power through His Spirit, His name, and His word. He continues to take an active, personal interest in the affairs of His people. He personally rules in their lives. He personally guides them and controls what happens to them. He personally gives words and wisdom for witnessing. He personally brings others across their paths so they too "might hear a message by which they would be saved."[30] He personally oversees the advance of His church. In short, the exalted Lord Jesus is with us always, in power, even "to the end of the age."[31]

Which Bible verses that speak of Jesus' personal involvement in our lives with His presence and power are your favorites? Why so?

How has your awareness of Jesus' presence, power, and personal involvement in your life been changed by this part of the study?

1 John 13:33, 36 **2** Matthew 28:20 **3** Luke 21:12 **4** Luke 21:14-15 **5** Acts 6:10-11 **6** Acts 16:14 **7** Acts 18:9-10 **8** The story of Ananias and Sapphira will be taken up in Chapter 9 **9** My thoughts on the various ways in which the Lord's presence is mediated in the Book of Acts were developed out of my reading "The Character and Purpose of Luke's Christology" by Douglas Buckwalter. **10** Acts 12:7,11 **11** Acts 12:21 **12** Acts 12:23 **13** Acts 12:23a **14** Acts 12:23b **15** Acts 12:24 **16** Acts 10:1-6 **17** Acts 11:14 **18** Acts 3:2 **19** Acts 3:6 **20** Acts 3:7-8 **21** Acts 4:5 **22** Acts 4:7 **23** Acts 19:14 **24** Acts 19:11, 13 **25** Acts 19:15 **26** Acts 19:16 **27** Acts 19:17 **28** Acts 3:14, 21 **29** Acts 4:8-10 **30** Acts 11:14 **31** Matthew 28:20

Exalted LORD

I do desire to live for You
Exalted One, Your will to do
Let my frail heart stay within Your grasp
And find in You a hope steadfast

I give my home, I give my life
For You to mold, for You to write
Surrendered now to a life complete
Filled with Your pow'r, laid at Your feet

I will obey and I'll believe
Your Word of truth spoken to me
And in the hour it is put to test
In You alone, I'll find my rest

Lyrics from "A Life Complete"
by Amy Branson Fata

9

LIVING UNDER
THE LORDSHIP OF JESUS

Human history turned a corner when Jesus ascended to the right hand of the Father and became the exalted Lord of lords. We now live in the age of His exaltation, an age that will continue until the day He comes again and "delivers the kingdom to God the Father" after destroying "every rule and every authority and power."[1] In the meantime, the reality of Jesus' exaltation is to be the dominating theme of our lives. We are to live and minister with our hearts and minds "set on things that are above, where Christ is seated at the right hand of God."[2] This means turning our backs on all aspects of life outside the realm of the Lord's presence and rule, "so that Christ will be exalted" in our bodies, "whether by life or by death."[3]

The Apostle Paul's determination to make his life a showcase for the exaltation of the Lord Jesus seems foreign to many modern-day professing Christians. Some even conclude: "A passion for the Lord like Paul's is not possible for someone like me. I'm just not that spiritual." Unfortunately, their conclusion leaves them lagging behind in "pressing on to make it their own."[4] They live in defeat and powerlessness, rather than "abundantly" as Jesus promised.[5]

Testing the Lord

Life outside the realm of Jesus' Lordship is no life at all. It is only an existence in the realm of death, something Ananias and Sapphira found out the hard way.[6] Ananias and Sapphira were among the believers in Jerusalem reported to be "one in heart and soul."[7] Like Barnabas and others, they sold their property and entrusted the proceeds to the administration of the apostles. However, Ananias and Sapphira held back a portion for themselves, conspiring to lie to the apostles about the amount they received from the sale. When Peter called attention to their lie, both "fell down and breathed their last."[8]

During the confrontation, Peter accused Ananias of lying "to the Holy Spirit" and ultimately "to God."[9] Sapphira came in "about three hours" later and embraced the lie told by her husband, prompting Peter to inquire: "How is it that you have agreed to test the Spirit of the Lord?"[10]

The sin of testing the Lord hearkens back to the experience of Israel at Rephidim.[11] There the Israelite community complained to Moses about not having any water to drink, arguing with Moses over whether the Lord was truly present among them to provide for their needs. Israel had seen the hand of the Lord separate the waters of the Red Sea for their escape from Pharaoh and his chariots in hot pursuit. They had experienced the Lord's healing of the bitter waters of Marah. They had eaten their fill of manna, the bread from heaven, each morning for more than a month. But now, at Rephidim, when they became thirsty, they grumbled against Moses, demanding to know "Is the Lord among us or not?"[12]

It was a ridiculous question. After all the Lord had done for them, the people had the audacity to cast doubt on His presence and ability to provide. The people became unwilling to wait on the Lord to meet their need, choosing instead to take Moses hostage and threatening to "stone" him if he did not prove then and there that the Lord was among them.[13] Exasperated, Moses humbly appealed to the Lord. "I will stand there before you there on the rock at Horeb," the Lord answered Moses. "strike the rock, and water will come out of it, and the people will drink."[14]

The Lord showed mercy that day at Rephidim and graciously taught Israel a valuable lesson about responding to His presence by faith: When you embrace the presence and power of the Lord by faith, there is life overflowing, abundant life, life to the full.

Danger

Unfortunately, Israel failed to learn the lesson. They continued to test the presence and power of the Lord, provoking Him to show them just how dangerous that can be. In one case, a great plague broke out among the people.[15] In another, "fire from the Lord burned among the people and consumed some outlying parts of the camp."[16] It seems that putting the Lord's presence and power to the test can provoke Him to prove the converse of the original lesson: When you reject the presence and power of the Lord, there is judgment and death overflowing. Indeed, the Lord is willing to demonstrate His presence and power by striking down those who refuse to believe.

Ananias and Sapphira foolishly brought on the danger of testing the exalted Lord's presence. They were fully aware that the Lord had authorized the apostles to represent Him in a unique way during the early years of His exaltation. The Lord had also equipped the apostles for this mission with the indwelling presence of the Holy Spirit, empowering them to be His "witnesses."[17] Ananias and Sapphira tested the reality of this arrangement by lying to the apostles. They became troubled over whether or not the Holy Spirit was truly present in the apostles, calling into question whether or not the apostles could be trusted to meet their needs should problems arise after the sale of their property and the distribution of the proceeds:

"Is the Lord truly present through the Holy Spirit in the apostles?"

Doubt led to Ananias and Sapphira conspiring to hold back a portion of the sale, which meant lying to the apostles, which meant also lying to the Holy Spirit, which meant also lying to

God, and ultimately to the exalted Lord Himself. Thus Ananias and Sapphira tested the Spirit of the Lord, asking the same question through their unbelief that Israel asked at Rephidim, "Is the Lord among us or not?" The Lord answered Ananias and Sapphira by showing His presence to everyone, not patiently and with some miraculous provision of life as at Rephidim, but rather in judgment and with overflowing death as on the other occasions.

"Great fear came upon the whole church" when they heard of Ananias and Sapphira's demise.[18] Their deaths illustrated in the clearest way possible that the exalted Lord Jesus was present in power through the Holy Spirit and the apostles. Their deaths also illustrated what anyone else might expect from attempts to live outside the realm of the exalted Lord's presence and rule embraced from the heart by faith—not life to the full, but certain death.

Read Psalms 78 and 106.
Note the verses that refer to Israel's experiences with testing the presence of the Lord. What observations can you make from these psalms?

Read 1 Timothy 5:6. How would you describe the life of someone who is "dead even while he or she lives"?

Describe what it feels like to doubt the presence of the Lord. What specific steps can be taken to counteract a failure to sense His presence and the feelings that go with such?

Under Satan's Control

When Peter confronted Ananias, he marveled at first, "Why has Satan has filled your heart to lie to the Holy Spirit and to keep back for yourself part of the proceeds of the land?"[19] To be filled with something in biblical contexts means to be under its control. Ananias somehow had come under the control of Satan, the ultimate challenger to the presence and power of the exalted Lord.

The spiritual realm over which Satan rules is the only alternative to the realm ruled by the Lord Jesus. If people do not choose to bring their hearts by faith under the rule of the exalted Lord Jesus, they choose by default to live under the control of Satan. They choose to exist under the control of his values, his philosophies, and his teachings, perhaps even under the direct control of Satan himself.

After Ananias and Sapphira were buried, the apostles performed "many signs and wonders among the people."[20] As a result, crowds of people, including some from the towns surrounding Jerusalem, were healed of illness and tormenting evil spirits, and an abundance of people "were added to the Lord."[21] But "the high priest and all his associates did not like what they saw, being themselves filled with jealousy."[22] Since jealousy has long been associated with Satan and his primordial rebellion against God, saying that the high priest and the others were filled with jealousy is tantamount to saying they were filled with Satan, just like Ananias and Sapphira. The high priest and his associates had unwittingly chosen to live under the control of the wrong lord. The jealousy that filled them simply made it obvious.

Life to the Full

The high priest and his associates "arrested the apostles and put them in the public prison."[23] They strictly charged the apostles at that time "not to teach in this name"; that is, in the Name of the Exalted Lord Jesus. Nevertheless, an angel of the Lord appeared before the apostles during the night. The angel "opened the prison doors and brought them out."[24] Then he told them: "Go and stand in the temple and speak to the people all the words of this life."[25]

The apostles had to choose: Do we submit to the lordship of Satan working through the high priest and his associates or do we submit to the exalted Lord Jesus?

The apostles chose to return to preaching: "And when they heard this, they entered the temple at daybreak and began to teach."[26] When the high priest caught up with them for the second time, he demanded to know why they had disobeyed his orders. They replied without hesitation, Peter taking the lead: "We must obey God rather than men! The God of our Fathers raised Jesus, whom you killed by hanging him on a tree. God exalted him at his right hand as Leader and Savior, to give repentance to Israel and forgiveness of sins. And we are witnesses to these things, and so is the Holy Spirit, whom God has given to those who obey him."[27]

Peter's answer calls attention to the presence, power, and authority of all three Persons of the Trinity. God the Father raised Jesus and exalted Him to His own right hand. Jesus is both Prince and Savior. And the Holy Spirit is a witness to it all. In effect, Peter tells the high priest and his associates: "The Holy Spirit was given to us when we obeyed the instructions of the exalted Lord. He is present with us now as at the beginning to be witnesses of these things. We are not about to stop obeying Him now. We choose rather to live in the reality of His presence, power, and authority."

The high priest and his associates eventually released the apostles, but not before flogging them for their insolence and repeating the demand to stop preaching in Jesus' Name. Getting flogged for choosing to live in the reality of the exalted Lord Jesus' presence and under his rule hardly seems like life to the full. However, the apostles...

"...left the presence of the council, rejoicing that they were counted worthy to suffer dishonor for the name. And every day, in the temple and from house to house, they did not cease teaching and preaching Jesus as the Christ."[28]

Life to full is still possible even during times of suffering when someone chooses to live under the Lord's rule. The presence and power of the exalted Lord makes it possible to carry on and to live with joy. Even a bad day lived under the rule of Jesus in His exaltation is better than a good day lived under the rule of Satan. Living under the Lord's rule and in His presence and power makes it possible for believers to see kingdom results from their lives and ministries and relationships. The realm of the Lord's presence is the realm of His abounding grace, the realm wherein His enemies are defeated and the lives of his people are sustained with His power and grace. The Apostle Paul expressed it this way:

"And God is able to make all grace abound to you, so that having all sufficiency in all things at all times, you may abound in every good work."[29]

How does what Jesus said in Matthew 5:10 and 6:33 apply to the theme of this lesson?

Describe in your own words what difference the presence of Jesus makes in your life?

How would you advise someone to develop a sense of the Lord's presence in his or her life?

What About You?

In the end, the modern-day use of the title "Lord" hardly seems adequate to describe all that Jesus is. Even when the title is expanded to "Lord of lords," it still can be difficult to fully grasp all it contains. Nevertheless, "Lord" and "Lord of lords" are the titles we find in Scripture, given to Him whose Name is above every name. The question is, knowing now what we know about Him, will we confess and bend the knee, or will we resist, or worse yet, turn away? We must choose, as did Paul, when he declared: "I count everything as loss because of the surpassing worth of knowing Christ Jesus my Lord."[30]

Jesus once said, "No one can serve two masters."[31] He made this declaration to signal the importance of living every moment of our lives in awareness of and responsiveness to His presence and power as the exalted Lord of lords. Other masters may offer the world, but in the end they cannot deliver. Only the exalted Lord Jesus is worthy of investing all that we are and have in Him. No wonder Paul chose to discount the value of everything else for the sake of gaining Christ. No wonder he chose to confess Him and to pursue the investment of a life lived under His exalted Lordship.

What about you? What is your heart telling you to retain or to give away? What is your heart prompting you to confess and pursue with all you are and have?

*How would you answer someone who said: "If I put Jesus first
in my life with my finances (or talents or time), I won't be able to live"?*

*Exactly what is your heart prompting you to confess and pursue
in regard to Jesus as the exalted Lord of lords?*

1 1 Corinthians 15:24 **2** Colossians 3:1-2 **3** Philippians 1:20 **4** Philippians 3:12 **5** John 10:10 **6** Acts 5:1-11 **7** Acts 4:32
8 Acts 5:10 **9** Acts 5:3-4 **10** Acts 5:9 **11** Exodus 17:1-17 **12** Exodus 17:7 **13** Exodus 17:4 **14** Ibid. **15** Numbers 11:33
16 Numbers 11:1 **17** Acts 1:8 **18** Acts 5:11 **19** Acts 5:3 **20** Acts 5:12 **21** Acts 5:14 **22** Acts 5:17 (NIV) **23** Acts 5:18
24 Acts 5:28 **25** Acts 5:19 **26** Acts 5:20 **27** Acts 5:29-32 **28** Acts 5:29 **29** 2 Corinthians 9:8 **30** Philippians 3:8
31 Matthew 6:24

FINAL WORD

As this book is being readied for publication, I am preaching through a series of studies on "The Kingdom of God" at the church where I pastor. God is a King, and He made the earth to be a place where His rule would be fully honored and obeyed. However, through original sin, the earth became a place of rebellion instead. So God launched His plan to restore the earth as a place where His rule is fully honored and obeyed. The Lord Jesus is at the center of that plan. His present session at the right hand of the Father will last until the moment of His return to establish His Kingdom with His physical presence here on earth in triumph over all His enemies. And "then comes the end, when he delivers the kingdom to God the Father after destroying every rule and every authority and power" (1 Corinthians 15:24). In the meantime, the exalted Lord Jesus has captured my heart. With heart-deep love and faith in Him, with profound gratitude and joy unspeakable, I willingly bend my knees and confess with my mouth, "Jesus is Lord!"

I pray that He captures your heart too, for He is "the Lamb who was slain" and He is "worthy to receive power and wealth and wisdom and might and honor and glory and blessing!" (Revelation 5:13).

Jesus is Lord!

About the Author

Randal L. Gilmore has served as the Senior Pastor of Hamilton Hills Baptist Church in Fishers, Indiana, since 1993. He is currently enrolled in doctoral studies in conflict management at Trinity Seminary in Newburgh, Indiana. Randal and his wife, Dale, have been married for more than 32 years. They are the blessed parents of five sons: Edward, Eric, Evan, Everett, and Elliott, along with two daughters-in-law, Kara and Mariah, and three grandchildren: Ean, Lydia, and MercyKate.

Other Books by the Author

"Where Do We Go From Here: The Path to Biblically Resolving Conflict"—"Where Do We Go" provides practical help for pastors, church leaders, married couples, business partners, and others with a simple, but powerful 8-step process for resolving conflict biblically. Inside "Where Do We Go", you'll find resources for making higher quality and more sophisticated group decisions during times of conflict. You will gain satisfaction in the end from solving problems without all the usual strife. "Where Do We Go" is available both in digital and print formats.

Other Titles Available from EXALT PUBLICATIONS:

"Why Am I So Afraid: Walking With God Through Fear and Anxiety?" by Steve Rowe

"Did I Say The Right Thing: Responding Well To Those Who Grieve" by Mitch A. Schultz

EXALT Publications is devoted to acknowleding, celebrating, and spreading the Good News of Jesus Christ's exaltation as Lord of lords. *"Exalted Lord"* draws on material from the Gospel of Luke and the Book of Acts to focus attention on the humiliation of Jesus Christ followed by His exaltation. *"Exalted Lord"* can be accompanied by a musical CD featuring Amy and Patrick Fata.

17584752R00057